Taking
the Waters
A Swim Around
Hampstead Heath

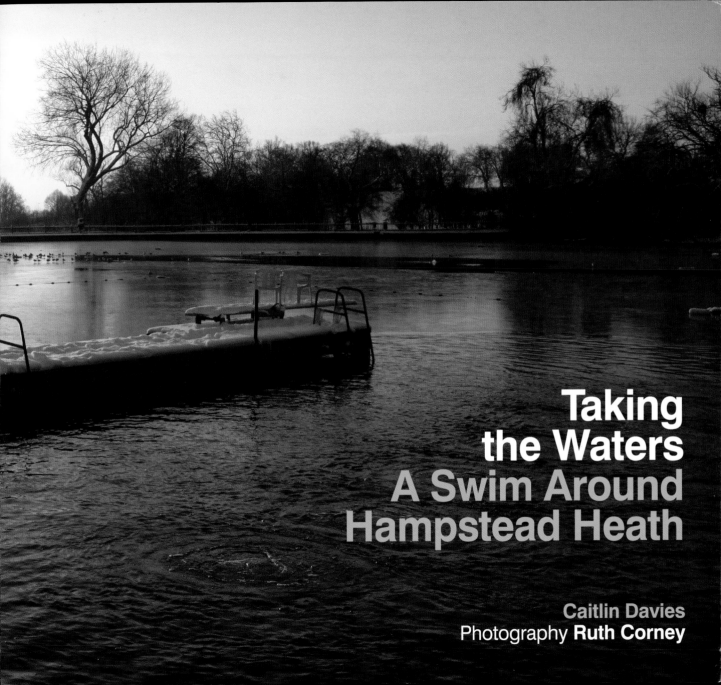

Taking the Waters
A Swim Around Hampstead Heath

Caitlin Davies
Photography **Ruth Corney**

To Lilah, Joe and Ruby, and to all swimmers; past, present and future…

CITY OF LONDON

Frances Lincoln Limited
www.franceslincoln.com

Taking the Waters: A Swim Around
Hampstead Heath
Copyright © Frances Lincoln Limited 2012
Text copyright © Caitlin Davies 2012
All photographs © Ruth Corney 2012
www.ruthcorney.com
Except where otherwise specified on page 173

First Frances Lincoln edition 2012

A catalogue record for this book is available from the British Library.

978-0-7112-3238-9

Printed and bound in China

1 2 3 4 5 6 7 8 9

In addition to the 150 open spaces within the square mile, the City of London owns and manages over 10,000 acres of parks and open spaces in and around London as part of its commitment to sustaining a world class city. Each open space is a unique resource managed for the use and enjoyment of the public and for the conservation of wildlife and historic landscape. The City of London's commitment to open spaces dates back to the 1870s, when, in response to the rapid disappearance of many public open areas to make way for the building of new suburban homes and city offices, it embarked on an ambitious project to safeguard some of what remained. Parks and open spaces managed by the City of London include Hampstead Heath, Epping Forest, Burnham Beeches, Ashstead Common, West Ham Park, Queen's Park and Highgate Wood.

Page 1 A gosling on the deck of the Ladies' Pond, with its parent close by, May 2011

Pages 2–3 Braving the snow, early on a February morning 2009

Right Flying at the lido, summer 2006

Contents

LEGEND

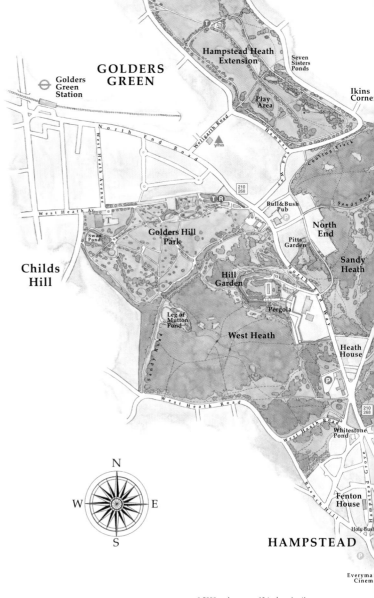

P PARKING

T TOILETS

R REFRESHMENTS: CAFES

P PUBS

MEADOWS / GRASS AREA

TREES / WOODS

PONDS / WATER

TENNIS COURTS

CP CHILDRENS' PLAY AREAS

FOOTBRIDGE

FENCED AREA

BUILDINGS

STEPS

ENGLISH HERITAGE BOUNDARY

GRAVEL PATH

PAVED PATH

FOOTPATH

ROAD

STREAM

RAILWAY

BICYCLE PATH

S SCULPTURE

★ POST OFFICE

RAILWAY STATION

UNDERGROUND STATION

C2 214 BUSES

yha YOUTH HOSTEL

1:5000 scale approx 12 inches=1 mile

METERS 0   100   200   300   400   500

FEET 0   500   1000   1500

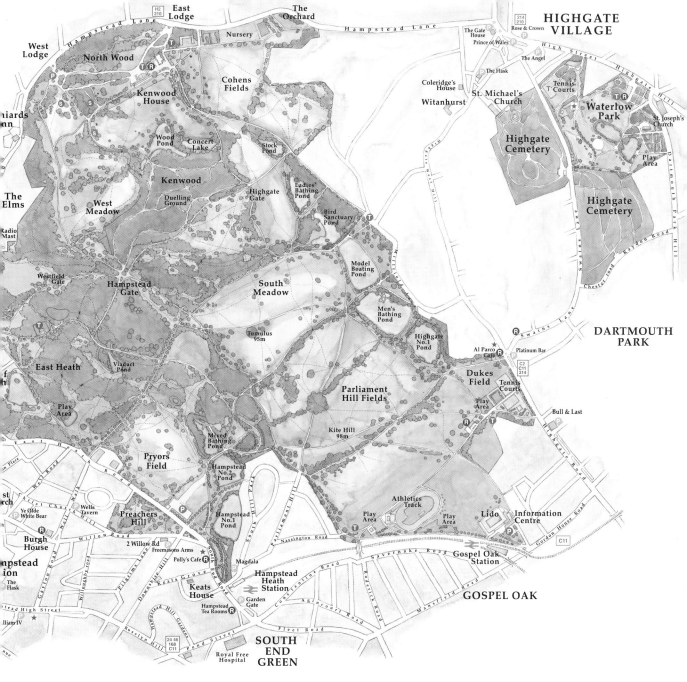

Introduction

It's a late Thursday afternoon in June and the path to the Kenwood Ladies' Bathing Pond is empty, its uneven surface dappled with shadow from the overhanging branches of ancient chestnut trees. To the right are grand Highgate houses hidden behind large walls, to the left is a mess of brambles, nettles and holly bushes, while above the foliage is so lush it almost obscures the sky. I come to a sign: 'Ladies Only – No Men Beyond This Point' and as I walk through the entrance there's a sudden burst of sunshine and the sounds of the outside world slip still further away.

On the right is a meadow where a handful of women sit in the sun. This is an area for peace and tranquillity, explains a sign, there are to be no children under eight and no mobile phones. Further down the path, on the left, is a deserted table tennis area and then a smaller, sloping lawn. There are only two women here; one is fully dressed with soaking wet hair, eating ravenously from a Tupperware box, the other wears a bikini and is busy with a reel of bright pink wool.

I head for the pond, an area of water shaped like the curved head of a spade. It's enclosed with bushes and reeds and, in some parts, densely packed trees. 'This is as warm as it will get,' a woman comments as I step a little cautiously down the metal steps. The average water temperature at this time of year is around 18°C.

There is something thrilling about dipping into a pond, the fact that it feels bottomless, that the water is so dark you can't see your body or what might lie underneath. I am acutely conscious of breaking the murky surface, of stepping in and being submerged. There is no chlorine here, no fear of stinging eyes. But there is a smell, an undercurrent of something damp and old, like wet bracken.

Right The entrance to the Kenwood Ladies' Bathing Pond on a summer's afternoon

Following page The beautiful, tranquil setting of the Ladies' Pond, viewed from the deck

The Ladies' Pond is the only wild swimming spot reserved just for women and girls (over eight) in the UK, if not Europe

It might be summer but the water feels cold and I need to keep moving. A coot swims by with a twig in its beak; another has made a nest in one of the lifebuoys. I can see the bobbing heads of eight women, hear smatterings of conversation. Far away comes the bark of a dog; an aeroplane hums in the sky and is gone. On a day like this there is a politeness about the pond, a feeling of being undisturbed. I swim through shadows, through areas of cold and spots of warmth, towards the shallower end where the mud is deep. Eventually I return to the steps and stand on the concrete jetty next to the lifeguards' hut, where a notice board is covered with newspaper clippings and poems, an explanation on the benefits of cold-water swimming, adverts for Reiki lessons and Egyptian dance classes.

The open top changing room is sparse and freshly swept, a single coat hanger balances from a hook, a canoe paddle lies against the wall. A notice advertises latex socks for 'ladies whose feet get cold'. A woman comes in; she's telling her companion she's been coming here for fifty years. She says it's not worth going away on holiday when you could come here. Her companion agrees, she says on a summer's day there is something magical, even biblical about this pond.

The Kenwood Ladies' Pond on Hampstead Heath is the only wild swimming spot solely for women – with women only lifeguards – in the UK, if not Europe. Opened to the public in 1926, its existence still tends to be spread by word of mouth. The pond has been a sanctuary for swimmers and topless sunbathers, lesbians and straights, everyday people and international film stars. On a hot summer's day thousands of women queue here to swim, while on bitter winter mornings around a dozen regulars, many pensioners, turn up at opening time for their daily bathe.

Men have their own pond too. It is an overcast Saturday lunchtime at the Highgate Men's Pond, just a short walk away along Millfield Lane; one of the spots where Romantic poet John Keats is said to have listened to the nightingales and stopped to chat with Samuel Taylor Coleridge. A side entrance leads through a wooden gate and down an overgrown path; it isn't as pretty as the Ladies' Pond, but there's still a feeling of a secret route to a reclusive place. Only on exceptional occasions are women allowed in.

Lifeguard Terry Turner shows me into his office, a wooden hut cluttered with papers and files and computer equipment. Above his desk is a black and white photograph, a group of sturdy men in shorts. The picture is around forty years old; the men are wrestlers, weightlifters, runners and gymnasts. Terry points at each man in turn, 'Dead, dead, dead.'

Then he stops and points to the man on the far left, 'He's still around though.' In comes Chris Maguire, in his seventies and still a boulder of a man, fresh from his daily swim.

Maguire is a member of the Highgate Life-Buoys, a swimmers' club founded in 1903, ten years after the Highgate Men's Bathing Pond opened. The members have their own hut, where outside on the cement an elderly man is doing yoga. Inside are a couple of grey plastic school chairs, a sink and a kettle. On the wall is a faded photocopy of a postcard signed by Charles F. Mauritzi, a famous Swedish diver. It shows him performing a swallow dive here in the early 1900s, when diving displays at the pond drew crowds of 70,000.

A wooden bench lines the room; exercise pulleys hang from a hook. On the bench is a single towel, a sandwich wrapped in cellophane and an unopened tin of sardines. In the corner sits Al Alvarez, poet, poker player and former mountaineer. The eighty one-year-old has swum all year round for ten years. He's joined by an ex-Labour councillor, a former member of a boy band from the 1950s, and then a body builder who undresses to

A SWALLOW-DIVE BY MR. MAURITZI AT HIGHGATE.

reveal tanned limbs and tight Speedos. There's camaraderie among the men, and a pride in the generally Spartan atmosphere. 'As you get older,' says Alvarez, as he thoughtfully dries himself, 'the horizon shuts in on you and the things you can do are more and more limited. It has saved my life, this pond.'

In the distance, down the pathway from the huts, comes the splash of a man diving into the water. The pond is vast compared to the Ladies' and although it's quiet today, it attracts over 130,000 visits a year. Men come from all walks of life. Alf Masterson, one of London's last 'totters' or rag and bone men, used to swim with a cigar in his mouth, Lord Phillips of Worth Matravers, President of the UK's Supreme Court, still cycles here daily to bathe. The absence of clothes is a great leveller, says one regular, 'crooks and coppers, intellectuals and wrestlers, Cabinet Ministers and boxers, Orthodox Jews and Muslims, we're all pals.' A portion of the changing room is the only place in London where nude sunbathing is allowed, while the lawn outside, to the displeasure of some regulars, is one of the best-known gay cruising spots in the capital. But for those who want to swim in mixed company, there is a third pond on Hampstead Heath.

Left The Mixed Pond is the oldest official bathing spot on Hampstead Heath

The Mixed Pond is a fifteen-minute walk away, near South End Green. The smallest of the three ponds, it was the first official bathing spot on Hampstead Heath, and men, women and children have been swimming here for over 200 years. It has been home to an Edwardian swimming club and to champion Channel swimmers; today it is most popular with families and tourists.

The women's changing area resembles a large bike shed; with corrugated walls and dark cubicles covered in cobwebs. It is 9 a.m. on a cloudy summer's day and there is just one person in the water, its surface scattered with midges.

I come down the steps, and launch myself in, swimming past three geese on the bank. Further away, in the fishing area, two dogs leap in and out of the water. People constantly cross the causeway that separates this pond from the adjacent fishing pond. Two men stop and look through binoculars; they are looking at the geese but I feel like I am part of the pond life. It isn't as tranquil here – I can hear the clanging of scaffolding and the noise of a tractor in the lane on the left. In the summer months, the only season this pond is now open to the general public, it can get very crowded. But today I am the only person in this freshwater pond just four miles from Trafalgar Square.

It's rarely tranquil at the Parliament Hill Lido, the fourth swimming spot on Hampstead Heath. It's 10 a.m. on a Sunday and in front of the low art deco building there is a queue of seventy people. The early morning swimmers have already been and gone and now it's the second intake of the day. Church bells toll from across the Heath, the metal shutter goes up with a rattling sound, and a day at the lido begins, just as it has since 1938 when the pool was built during the heyday of swimming glamour. Today people rush in, weighed down with picnics, towels, drinks and newspapers. Minutes later everyone has grabbed a spot, many heading for the cement steps that rise like a mini amphitheatre beside the pool. You could be on the top deck of an ocean liner here, a boat moored temporarily on a field in north London.

The surface of the 60m pool is gleaming; the sun reflecting off the new stainless steel bottom that shimmers like a silver skin. At the poolside the temperature is 21°C, and it's the same in the water. Six lifeguards, in bright yellow t-shirts and red shorts, patrol the edge, whistles at the ready. Families dominate the shallow end, groups of teenagers the deeper end, others attempt laps. Two ducks ride the waves, their necks as purple as peacock feathers. Parliament Hill Lido is not a secret place, instead life is louder here and in some ways more democratic. But while the air is full of splashing, squeals and laughter, the sound is still oddly muted, seeming to evaporate up into the open air.

Inside the café the light is dim and the air heavy with the smell of damp pastry. Children queue for ice creams. Metal trays offer two sausage rolls and a single slice of cake. In the staff office on the other side of the pool Paul Jeal, senior swimming facilities supervisor, is keeping a careful eye on CCTV footage on a screen on the wall. Swimmers walk past outside, admiring themselves in the one-way glass. A voice comes over the tannoy, 'Paul, do you want your breakfast now?' He accepts a poached egg, still not taking his eyes from the CCTV screens. When the lido is full to capacity, as it will be today when 2,500 people are expected, everyone's alert. Life at the lido has seen a revival since recent refurbishments, and in winter it is one of only two unheated outdoor pools in the capital. Seventy years ago London was a 'City of Lidos', today Parliament Hill is one of the very few to have survived.

Right Parliament Hill Lido was built during the heyday of swimming glamour, today it's one of only two unheated outdoor pools left open in London

Below Inside the lifeguard's office staff keep a close eye on CCTV footage, the dark interior providing a stark contrast to the bright scene outside
Right Escaping a sticky London day in the refreshing waters of the lido, circa 2004

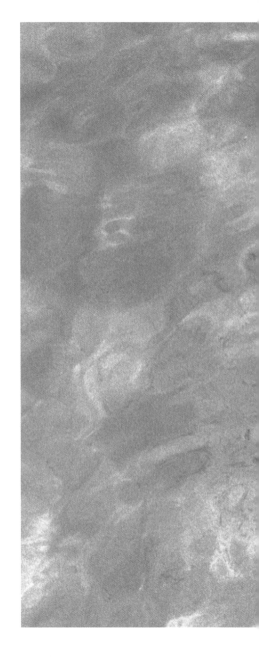

The four swimming places on Hampstead Heath are all in their own way unique, and the three ponds and the lido are inextricably linked with the history of swimming and sunbathing, life saving and diving in the UK. Today they are managed by the City of London Corporation, the current guardians of Hampstead Heath, and share the same lifeguards. Many swimmers use both the ponds and the lido, varying where they swim depending on the time of year or ease of access. A group of committed, and often elderly, outdoor bathers swim daily, braving rain, ice and snow, just for the pleasure of a dip in the waters of Hampstead Heath.

The Men's and Ladies' Ponds are the only lifeguarded, open-water swimming places in the UK to be open every day of the year. They have been celebrated in art, fiction, poetry and film; but they have also sparked petitions, protest and demonstrations. Their history is long and glorious, but fraught with conflict. Should men and women be allowed to swim together? What about topless sunbathing

and nudism? Is swimming in cold-water ponds inherently dangerous? Just whom do these places 'belong' to and does anyone have the right to change them?

Questions like these have sparked numerous battles over the years, battles which have been played out at the ponds, through the pages of the local and national press, in church halls, courtrooms, the grand surroundings of Guildhall and the Houses of Parliament. Ever since the ponds were first dug, bathers have come head to head with the various Heath managers, initially demanding that swimming be better regulated, and then more recently fighting just as furiously for de-regulation. Many of today's bathers see themselves as free spirits, demanding the right to swim when and how they like, resisting bureaucratic controls imposed from above and refusing to bow to the government cult of health and safety and all the restrictive legislation this implies.

In 2005 swimmers fought a determined battle against the shortening of hours, the introduction of charges and the possibility of closure. The same year a landmark court case established the individual's right to take risks by allowing a group of winter bathers to swim at the Mixed Pond without lifeguards.

It was a challenge to research and write this book, when much of the history has never been written down. It has often been hard to establish the truth, even over events that occurred as recently as twenty years ago, and anecdotal evidence can be tainted by politics, both internal and external. Swimmers love their bathing spots and will do all they can to keep them. There is a sense of ownership among some long time bathers, and people can be cautious and even suspicious about 'outsiders'. No one wants these places to become overrun, but if they aren't used then they won't survive.

Each swimming place has its own stories to tell. How and why did they come to be, and how long will they continue to exist?

1.
The Birth of the Ponds

'There sat the man who had traced to their source the mighty ponds of Hampstead, and agitated the scientific world with his Theory of Tittlebats.'
Charles Dickens, Pickwick Papers, *1837*

The bathing ponds on Hampstead Heath have a long and confusing history and Samuel Pickwick Esq is not the only one to have wondered about their source. Modern maps show twenty nine ponds scattered over these 320 hectares of land, and many are linked and flow into each other. On the eastern side of the Heath, reaching up towards Highgate, is a string of five ponds, which includes the Ladies' and the Men's. To the south, leading down to Hampstead Heath Station, is a string of three ponds, including the Mixed. But over the years as the Heath has expanded and ownership and management changed, new ponds have been created and others drained or filled in. Maps have been re-drawn, names have changed, and dates can be frustratingly hard to pin down.

The history of the Heath itself is one of a clash of interests, between those who wanted to sell, build on or enclose it, to erect houses, roads, and railways, and those who campaigned to keep it in its natural state for everyone to use.

And while today's swimming ponds may appear natural, they were artificially created, having been dug to provide water for London by damming two Heath streams. When rain falls on higher ground, which is made up of sand and gravel, it drains down to the lower layer of sandy clay and then to a layer of water-resistant London Clay. As the rainwater is forced to the surface again, so the streams are born. One begins near the Vale of Health, the other near Kenwood. The streams then join in Camden Town to form the River Fleet, which in turn flows through London and joins the Thames. The Fleet is one of the city's

Right The Heath ponds were places of great beauty to Constable who painted many in his countryside scenes, including this one of Branch Hill Pond in 1828

great 'lost' rivers, becoming gradually buried below ground when a new sewer system was built for London. Today it still flows beneath us, and the only sections which can be seen above ground are on Hampstead Heath.

There had been plans to tap these streams since Tudor times when, under the orders of Henry VIII, reservoirs were created to supply water for London. The city's Mayor had 'founde out dyvers great and plentyfull sprynges at Hampstede-heath', and in 1544 the London Conduit Act was passed, allowing the Corporation of the City of London to search, dig for and 'make heades and vautes' to convey fresh water to the city. For every spring on the Heath it would pay the Bishop of Westminster 'one pounde of pepper.'

The plan apparently failed. But in 1589 the Corporation came up with a scheme to draw the various springs 'into one head and course', and according to some Victorian historians, it was then that the ponds were made. But modern historians insist nothing happened until 1692 when the springs on the Heath were leased to the Hampstead Water Works Company and it made, or possibly enlarged, four ponds as reservoirs, some as early as 1703. These became the Hampstead Ponds. A 1748 map shows two ponds on the Lower Heath, another map fourteen years later shows four, and by 1810 this was down to three.

The Company also leased a farm at Millefieldes (later known as Millfield) and started work on another seven reservoirs, which became the Highgate Ponds – although some may have already existed in the seventeenth century. Some ten years later, the New River Company took over the lease on the springs. By then Hampstead had become an affluent suburb, populated initially by wealthy Londoners fleeing the plague and the Great Fire in the seventeenth century, then developing into a spa town in the eighteenth century when the local spring water was believed to have healing properties. Even today many bathers still believe the water of the ponds, dark and murky as it may be, has special qualities.

The Heath ponds have been used for bathing since at least the early 1800s, but the oldest official swimming spot is the Mixed Pond, one of today's three East Heath ponds. It has also been called Upper Hampstead Pond, Hampstead Pond No. 3 and the fourth pond. When William Blake in his 1804 poem Jerusalem refers to 'The Ponds where boys to bathe delight', he may well have had this pond in mind. The ponds were places of great beauty to John Constable too, and he painted several in his sweeping countryside scenes of the 1820s. This was a time, however, when few people actually knew how to swim. Both men and women bathed naked outdoors, although this was more of an immersion than a swim. 'Bathing is best performed when quite naked but decency forbids entire nudity', advised one commentator. But around the middle of the century things changed, swimming became a recognised sport and regular competitions were held by the National Swimming Society of Great Britain.

When the Baths and Washhouses Act was passed in 1846, local authorities were allowed to build public baths – for both swimming and washing – and the first in London opened three years later. As swimming became more popular, styles changed. While the doggie paddle had been common at the end of the 1700s, by the early nineteenth century it had been replaced by the breaststroke. Experiments with different leg movements led to the sidestroke, and eventually the trudgen style was introduced, thanks to swimmer John Arthur Trudgen who copied the technique off Native Americans, and this developed into the modern front crawl. By 1852, London's seven swimming baths, which held everything from animated fêtes to egg diving contests and pole walking competitions, attracted 800,000 bathers a year. In 1869 the Amateur Swimming Association was founded, with 300 member clubs.

While indoor swimming was becoming all the rage, outdoor swimming in freezing cold water was popular too. As early as 1702 physician Sir John Floyer had published a book on the history of cold bathing. In it he wrote, 'The Art of Cold Bathing was certainly first invented by the Common People who used it for the Preservation of their Heath.' He argued that cold-water bathing not only had a glorious history, but was good for the body, providing a cure for rickets and rheumatic-pains and putting new life into the elderly. By the 1800s cold-water bathing was generally seen as a cure for various ills, and while this usually meant a dip in the sea, many bathers chose rivers, lakes and ponds. In the 1850s a bathing lake was created at London's Victoria Park, while the Serpentine Swimming Club in Hyde Park, often described as the oldest open-air swimming club in the world, was formed in 1864. Its traditional Christmas Day race continues today.

So it is not surprising that the array of ponds on Hampstead Heath attracted plenty of unregulated swimming. But they could be dangerous, especially for those diving into shallow water. In the summer of 1844, a family party were enjoying a Sunday picnic near the Mixed Pond when one of the group went for a swim. The press reported, 'He had not gone three yards into the water when he sank in the presence of his family, and never rose again.' A few years later, a twenty-year-old 'expert swimmer and celebrated diver', leapt into the Mixed Pond, performing a somersault. He was found lying on the bottom, where it was only four feet deep, with his neck broken. The coroner said this should serve as a warning to others and as an inducement to the Lord of the Manor (Sir Thomas Maryon Wilson, who then owned the land) and to the New River Company to prevent it happening again. But happen again it did.

Every summer there were as many as four deaths a month. Some were accidental; but the Heath ponds also became known for a high number of suicides. The *Leeds Mercury* ran a story 'Love's Rebels' which opens with a gentleman standing at midnight by 'the Bathing Pond' on Hampstead Heath. Before long he is approached by the inevitable, a well-dressed young man about to throw himself in over a failed love affair.

It was concern over the number of fatalities that eventually led to the provision of proper bathing places. In the summer of 1871 a letter writer to *The Times* commented, 'Sir, – What a glorious opportunity now offers for forming an open-air swimming bath … On Hampstead Heath are several ponds, any one of them available for the purpose; the one called the fourth pond is at present used for bathing but it is in a very objectionable condition, having muddy banks and bottom, with no facility for dressing.' The pond was so dangerous that the local vestry had provided a man and a boat 'to guard as much as possible against accident.' The letter writer suggested one pond be properly bottomed, with walled sides and landing places, a deep part for swimmers and divers and a shallow part for learners. He also suggested charging a small fee for accommodation and towels, which would 'yield a good return, upon any sum expended.' While the facilities at the Mixed Pond were still non-existent, the idea of charging bathers had already begun.

Unlike many who still frowned on women swimming – whether indoors or out – the letter writer also suggested the pond be available for 'ladies as well as gentlemen', as long as they swam separately. Only a few indoor baths had pools for women then; others were segregated depending on the day, although in 1876 women did get the lake in Victoria Park to themselves, after men were given a new purpose built pool.

But when it came to public displays of daring underwater acts, it was often women who took centre stage. Natationists like Agnes Beckwith amazed audiences with their ability to submerge in plate glass aquariums for minutes at a time, where they would undress, write on slates, eat sponge cakes and drink bottles of milk. Beckwith, the daughter of a famed swimming professor, was also a serious long distance swimmer, but few women got the chance to show off their prowess, unless they took part in Barnum and Bailey spectaculars alongside a 'stupendous collection of new freaks and living curiosities'.

Right Agnes Beckwith, long distance swimmer and famed performer, appearing at the Royal Aquarium Westminster, in 1885

As well as safety fears at the Heath ponds, many frowned upon the continuing habit of naked bathing. 'Would proprietors of baths compel their patrons to wear drawers during the forthcoming season?' inquired *The Swimmer Magazine*. Men had had specific costumes for bathing from the 1840s; short legged drawers which originated in France and which were tied at the waist with string. By the 1870s a new one-piece costume was introduced – a short sleeved jersey with short legs – but most men continued to bath naked. This caused considerable horror to 'A Ratepayer' who wrote to *The Times* to describe strolling on the Heath at 6 p.m. on a Sunday afternoon only to come across 'some fifty perfectly naked men and boys bathing in the pond and running about the banks among the bystanders in a state of absolute nudity ... I have been more shocked and disgusted than I can find words to express.'

It wasn't just the nakedness, but the fact that the body of a young man had just been dragged out of the mud. The letter writer wanted to know why there were no regulations to restrict bathing within 'decent bounds of time and place', why dangerous ponds were left open 'without any means of preventing accidents or rescuing drowning people', and why the Metropolitan Board of Works allowed naked people to run around on a Sunday.

The Board of Works had been created in 1855, an appointed body to oversee the city's growth, and had only just agreed to take over parts of the Heath, following the death of Sir Wilson. The Lord of the Manor had been trying for decades to sell Heath land for development, a plan that was met with fierce opposition by local residents who waged a forty-year campaign through the Houses of Parliament. This is often described as one of the first great conservation battles of modern times, and it resulted in the formation of a Hampstead Heath Protection Fund Committee. When Wilson died, his heir sold about 220 acres of land to the Metropolitan Board of Works and the resulting Hampstead Heath Act of 1871 declared that the Board 'shall for ever keep the Heath open, unenclosed, and unbuilt on … and at all times preserve, as far as may be, the natural aspect and state of the Heath.'

But still nothing was done to provide proper swimming spots. 'This pleasure giving sport is increasing in popularity, we rejoice to say,' declared the *Penny Illustrated Paper* in 1874, 'Hampstead ponds could so easily be made into safe swimming-baths for the north of London.' The following year, when Captain Matthew Webb, greased with porpoise oil, became the first man to swim the Channel unaided, long distance swimming became glamorous and romantic. By now hundreds of swimming clubs had been formed across the country, lessons were beginning to be taught in schools, and London baths had sixteen different swimming clubs. But baths came at a cost; the St Pancras Baths in Camden for example cost two shillings a month. What better then, than to use a pond for free?

In 1884, local swimmer Robert Sandon discovered the Mixed Pond when he moved to Kentish Town. He later recalled, 'The only pond open for bathing was the one now used at Hampstead. …There was no bathing shed; no one dreamed of such a thing.…There was nothing but the natural bank of the pond, and that is where bathers had to undress, placing their clothes on mother earth.' But five years later, parish records refer to 'two ponds … which at stated hours are available for bathing' (which may refer to another pond on East Heath that was later filled in) and the Board of Works had now provided an attendant at the Mixed Pond, a Mr Ringe. Swimmers were allowed to dress in his hut, although the floor was rotten and the walls badly cracked. One bather wrote to the press to say he'd been 'anticipating a grand clear out and a well kept pond,' now the Board was in charge, 'Alas for human hopes!… A few pounds judiciously expended would put matters straight and greatly add to the comfort and safety of the bathers, who from May to August are to be counted in scores.'

Despite a dilapidated hut, a boat that was 'getting very crank' and plenty of pots, pans and tin ware lying at the bottom, the Mixed Pond was now hosting several sporting events, including an 800-yard swim and a Christmas Day race. In March 1884 a bather reported that swimming had been kept up throughout the winter, and on Christmas morning the water had been 'comparatively warm' and no one attempting 'the stake and back' had experienced any discomfort, aside from numb feet and hands.

But although more people than ever were swimming, there was still very little knowledge in how to rescue someone in danger of drowning, let alone resuscitate them. In the UK there were around 3,500 drownings a year in inland waters, while methods of trying to restore life – such as blowing air through one nostril with a pair of bellows – were downright dangerous. Then in 1891 champion swimmer William Henry formed the Swimmers' Life Saving Society, later to become the Royal Life Saving Society. It produced a life saving handbook, formed branches in England and Australia, and introduced the first life saving diploma. Its motto was *Quemcunque Miserum Videris Hominem Scias* – Whomsoever you see in distress recognise in him a fellow man. Henry, who is buried in Highgate Cemetery, was an English Salt Water Champion and Long Distance Champion. He wrote prolifically on the 'art' of swimming, and was also an expert Scientific Swimmer – the forerunner of modern synchronised swimming.

By the time Henry formed his life saving society, Hampstead Heath was swarming with people, with up to 100,000 on a fine bank holiday. One of the big draws was the fairground, erected seasonally near the Mixed Pond, and the advent of the railway in 1860 had made it all the easier to get to. Skating was popular too, and was far more organised and supervised than bathing, with revellers skating by moonlight and unemployed men paid to sweep the ice. But it wasn't just skaters who used the Mixed Pond in winter, swimmers did too. The pond's boatman reported 360 bathers in October 1892, and while this had dropped to 237 in December, the water had fallen to freezing point for over a week. On Christmas morning the pond was covered in ice three-quarters of an inch thick, but there were still five bathers. In January 1893 the pond remained largely frozen and it was difficult to keep a hole open in front of the diving board, yet there were still 210 bathers. One man, a Mr Mitschaneck, swam every morning over a six-month period, while another, a Mr M. Browne, missed his daily dip only once. This compelled one enthusiastic swimmer to write to the *Ham & High*, 'Think of this, ye lie-a-beds, sleeping the golden hours away until roused by the postman's knock.'

An Award of Merit from the RLSS, 1904

The Mixed Pond now had its own swimming club, the Highgate Water Rats, and the first proper bathing shed, built by the London County Council. The LCC, the first elected London-wide governing authority, had taken over responsibility for the Heath in 1889 after a major reorganisation of local government, during which the Metropolitan Board of Works had been abolished. The LCC appointed a new attendant at the Mixed Pond, William Pikesley – described as 'a thoroughly reliable man, always at his post, attentive and obliging' – who served as boatman. In 1893 he received an honorary award, inscribed on parchment, from the Humane Society for his 'courageous rescue from drowning of a would-be suicide'.

BATHING POND.   HAMPSTEAD HEATH LONDON.

Nice weather for this sort of place ? Do you know the Heath well, I've never been. Yours J.S.

Above A postcard of the Mixed Pond, circa 1911

Right The Mixed Pond became a favourite summertime resort for Londoners

The Humane Society had been formed in 1774 by two doctors who wanted to promote the then controversial technique of resuscitation. It was initially called the Society for the Recovery of Persons Appeared Drowned and it paid two guineas to anyone attempting a rescue in the Westminster area of London and four guineas to anyone successfully bringing someone back to life. But when this was exploited by those who pretended to drown while a friend supposedly saved them, monetary rewards were replaced with medals and certificates.

Boatman Pikesley wasn't the only one to win such an award at the Mixed Pond. In July 1890, a four-year-old boy fell into 'the large and deep bathing pond' and twelve-year-old Thomas Charles Barrett plunged in to rescue him, in seven feet of water. Barrett was later given a bronze medal, a certificate and twenty shillings from the Humane Society. At the award ceremony he was praised for being 'a very brave boy … your action was a noble and unselfish one. But virtue often brings its own reward when least expected.'

Now that the LCC was in charge, the Mixed Pond underwent something of a transformation in the last few years of the nineteenth century. In 1897 *Lloyd's Weekly Newspaper* praised the works undertaken by the Parks and Open Spaces Committee; 'The space reserved near the Hampstead bathing pond for the use of bathers has been converted into one of the prettiest spots imaginable, under the assiduous and intelligent care of boatman Pikesley. The path leading from the dressing room to the edge of the water is embowered with arches covered with canariensis, and all round is a veritable fairyland with the many hues of golden elder, autumn anemone, laurels, different kinds of privet and ivy, maples and willows.'

The LCC, it seemed, wanted to turn the Heath into a park, and set to work planting trees, trimming hedgerows and turning footpaths into roads. This infuriated local residents, who formed the Hampstead Heath Protection Society, known today as the Heath and Hampstead Society.

But the LCC's improvements were a success at the Mixed Pond and it soon became the 'cockney child's seaside'. Postcards of the time describe it as 'the favourite resort in the summertime for swimmers. It is only two minutes walk from Hampstead Heath station, but its beautiful rural position dismisses all consideration of the proximity of the great city.' On Thursdays the pond was now reserved for women, and 'the elegant costumes and swimming performances have become a local attraction.' The Mixed Pond was no longer the dangerous place it had once been; now it was a veritable fairyland, a treasured oasis in one of the fastest growing metropolises in the world. But pretty as it was, there was now another official bathing spot on the Heath; and it was the Highgate Men's Pond that would really put the ponds on the international map.

CHILDRENS PADDLING CORNER, HAMPSTEAD HEATH.
THE COCKNEY CHILD'S "SEA-SIDE"

WATER SPORTS IN THE BATHING PONDS AT HIGHGATE

DRAWN BY A. G. SMALL

2.
Highgate Men's Pond

Highgate Men's Pond – also known as Highgate No. 2 Pond and sometimes, confusingly, as Hampstead Bathing Pond – opened on 1 May 1893, with very little publicity at all. This worried Robert Sandon who in the late spring of 1893 had often stopped to watch LCC workers putting up a bathing shed, diving stage and platform. When Sandon turned up on opening day he found an attendant called Walter May in charge, 'a youngish chap' whose sea career had been cut short by injury, and an assistant, a 'rather extraordinary character' known as Tosh. But no public announcement had been made of the pond's opening. 'No newspaper knew of it, and friend May began to look a bit glum, as he was afraid if the public did not respond, the place would be closed. I took it upon myself to send a letter to the sporting press to let the public, and especially swimmers, know of the new facility they had for public healthful bathing in the open air, which was there for their use without fee or cost of any kind.'

Sandon's plan succeeded, and over the coming decades the pond became so popular, especially in hot summer months, that he feared some of the regulars wished it hadn't. Attendant May meanwhile, would become renowned for his watchfulness and bravery, often helping weakening swimmers into his boat. He would receive an award from the Royal Humane Society for conspicuous bravery in rescuing a would-be suicide, and would be credited with saving the lives of three children.

The Highgate Men's Pond, an impressive 110 yards in diameter, was part of a parcel of land, which, along with Parliament Hill, had been bought for the public in 1890 and added as an extension to the Heath, with the LCC having overall responsibility. The other two ponds were to be used for model yacht racing and dog paddling, and are still known today as the boat and the dog pond.

Prior to opening the Men's Pond was, according to the local press, 'lined with black mud at the shallow end where the boys enter', while the weeds were so thick 'as to be

Left An illustration from *The Graphic* in 1901 showing the bank of the Men's Pond packed with spectators

a source of positive danger.' Naked bathers were still seen as a problem, 'There is no shelter or screen sufficient to keep the bathers out of view of pedestrians … it is difficult to gauge the fibre of grown men who expose themselves before respectable women and young children when for a shilling a decent bathing costume can be bought.'

The LCC, concerned that the water was too deep, wanted only competent swimmers to use the pond, and only on summer mornings. But the hours set aside for bathing quickly became a source of dispute and the LCC seemed unaware that open-air swimming would prove so popular. A year after opening, a swimmer launched a petition to keep the pond open during winter, and more petitions followed until morning swimming was allowed throughout the year. In 1902 women were given sole use of the pond on Wednesdays, the LCC provided 'private dressing boxes' and Dorothy May, daughter of boatman May, was on hand to assist.

In 1903 the LCC agreed to open the pond all day on weekdays, but when this attracted 'loafers and other undesirable persons', bathing was stopped between 11 a.m. and 4 p.m., except for women on Wednesdays. Two years later, such was the desire for open-air swimming, that 900 male post office employees signed a petition asking for the pond to be re-opened all day in the summer. Again the LCC gave in, and around fifty people bathed regularly in the morning and afternoon. An illustration from *The Graphic* shows an idyllic summer scene of bonnet-ed ladies reclining on the bank, amid children and swans, watching a pond full of men somersaulting and diving.

Shortly after it opened, the Men's Pond began to attract a group of hardy year-round swimmers and winter bathing was being heralded, by *The Times* at least, as a 'heroic form of the Englishman's morning tub … these winter bathers are an inoffensive kind of lunatic, who harm nobody but themselves'. Robert Sandon described 'a number of lively young sparks' who regularly went in together and were known as the 'Barmy Club'. The Highgate Bathers, another in-formal group of swimmers, had started a Christmas morning race in 1895, and also established a life saving class, for which Sandon was an instructor. He was also president of the Amateur Swimming Club of England, honorary treasurer of the Amateur Swimming Association, and wrote numerous scien-tific papers on swimming techniques.

But it was the formation of the Highgate Life-Buoys in 1903 that would forever link the Men's Pond

673 HAMPSTEAD HEATH. — *View from Parliament Hill.* — LL.

with lifesaving. The club's stated aim was to promote methods of life saving and to assist the Life Saving Society (LSS) and the St John's Ambulance. Walter May appears to have been instrumental in the formation of the club, and there are photos of May with Professor Walter Brickett, an Olympic swimming instructor and one of the original founders of the LSS. According to May's great-grandson John Neal, 'the purpose of the Life-Buoys was life saving, healthy living, promoting swimming culture and entering the water without hesitation. You weren't to hesitate at the waterside thinking how cold it would be, that was the important bit.'

The Life-Buoys took over the running of the Christmas Day race, and eventually many of the summer competitions as well. The club's first president was Edmond Bryne, who in 1903 won the veterans Christmas race for the third time. By 1905 the Life-Buoys had around seventy members, and over the next two decades would receive eleven proficiency certificates and ten bronze medals from the LSS, as well as nine St John's Ambulance certificates for first aid.

Bryne was succeeded by William Mackenzie, an optician who lived in Highbury and who was known as 'Grandpa'. Everyday, he walked two miles from his home for a swim, 'very pointedly without touching the raft', according to Sandon, and then strode home for breakfast.

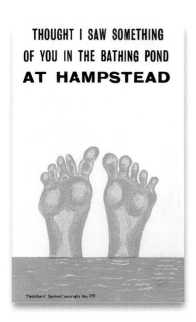

THOUGHT I SAW SOMETHING
OF YOU IN THE BATHING POND
AT HAMPSTEAD

Titchfield Series Copyright No 319

McKenzie took part in the club's winter sports until the age of ninety, and at his funeral in 1911 the club fittingly sent a wreath in the form of a lifebuoy.

The LCC was now fully aware of the popularity of the pond – which in 1905 hosted the mile championships of England – and made further improvements, enlarging the changing compound, draining the waterlogged path outside, and providing two floating rafts. In 1909 it cleaned the pond of several feet of mud, and numerous fish, including an 11lb pike, were transferred to other ponds.

But while the Highgate Men's Pond was popular with year-round bathers, it was for diving that it would become renowned. It was here that the LSS organised massive galas, featuring champion divers from all over the world and displays of life saving techniques by local school children and uniformed police – including the aptly named PC Innocent of Hornsey. Swimming entertainments were immense affairs, with racing, water polo matches, life saving displays, diving, and a brass band playing during the intervals. There were also exhibitions of ornamental swimming, which included imitating a torpedo, swimming like a duck, swimming crab fashion, and the rather tricky skill of swimming with both legs out of the water.

Diving displays at the Men's Pond drew huge crowds, and the diving stage that Sandon had watched being built, a firm board fixed at 15ft above the water, was the first professional, purpose built diving stage in England. 'The pond was chosen because of its depth,' explains Jim McNally, current president of the Great Britain Diving Federation, 'and because it was cheaper for the LCC to take advantage of an existing natural facility. It was quite a radical thing to build it.' Two years after the pond opened the LSS staged the first of twelve National Graceful Diving Championships where competitors (men only) performed standing and running plain dives from both the 15ft board and from a 33ft diving stage put up temporarily in the summer.

Diving had certainly come a long way since the early nineteenth century. Then a dive had been a more of a plunge and the aim was to dive in and go as far as possible underwater. But Swedish and German gymnasts developed diving into an art form until 'a dive' meant the actual process of entering the water. The Swedes also brought in the swan or swallow dive – far more graceful than the 'English header' – and fancy diving; adding more complex somersaults and twists. In 1904 diving for men became an Olympic sport when, at the St Louis games, a 10m platform diving event was introduced, as well as a 'plunge for distance'.

Famous Swedish divers like 'Messrs Hagborg, Mauritzi and Johansson' often attended galas at the Men's Pond. Otto Hagborg was an impressionist painter, and brother of the more successful artist August Hagborg. Charles Mauritzi was the diver whose picture remains on the wall in the Highgate Life-Buoys' hut today, while Carl Hjalmar August Johansson was a diver, swimmer and track and field athlete who competed in three Olympics, winning a gold medal in 1908 for the 10m platform event.

As a result of all the interest in diving, the Amateur Diving Association was formed, of which Sandon was an original member. Diving displays continued to feature heavily in LSS galas and in 1902 when King Edward VII was crowned, competitors came from the USA, France, Belgium and Sweden, and were watched by 30,000 spectators. By now the LSS had revised and re-issued its handbook, increased its number of branches, and awarded an array of shields and trophies. In 1904 it became the Royal Life Saving Society and its galas at the Men's Pond – a mixture of instruction, sport and entertainment – drew crowds of 70,000, with William Henry keeping everyone informed by megaphone. Thanks to the RLSS displays, people were now far better educated in life saving techniques. Men in the Royal Navy were instructed in life saving and classes for park keepers were held at London's public baths. In 1907

Top left Boatman Walter May (middle) with his sons, Christmas morning 1919

Bottom left Swimmers pose for a photograph after the traditional Christmas Day swim in 1916

Below A Highgate Life-Buoys badge

the RLSS formally adopted the 'Schafer' method of resuscitation, which meant laying the subject face down while 'the operator' either sat astride or on one side, applying pressure to the person's chest to drive the air and water out of the lungs.

In 1911 the winner of the King's Cup, held at the Men's Pond and awarded for proficiency in swimming and life saving, was E. G. Finlay of Australia. The contest was open to all amateurs who were required to carry out a rescue test over a distance of 440 yards 'fully clad with the exception of coat and waistcoat'. Such was the involvement of the Highgate Life-Buoys in promoting life saving that the RLSS awarded the club a silver gilt trophy.

By now women were diving at the Men's Pond as well and the Ladies Graceful Diving Competition was held here three times, beginning in 1911. One such diver was London born Isabelle Mary 'Belle' White, the captain of the Olympic women divers team, who practiced high dives at the Men's Pond. She won a bronze medal in the 10m platform event at the 1912 Olympics, the year women's diving was introduced, and went on to compete in three other Olympics.

The Highgate Men's Pond was now well and truly established on the international map, and the Heath had become 'a pleasure garden' for all of London. Postcards were produced celebrating the Men's Pond in the early 1900s when it was then so open – and unfenced – that on Wednesdays when women swam, crowds of men and children lined the banks to watch.

Even when World War I was declared in 1914, when an anti-aircraft station was built on Parliament Hill and troops practiced drills on the Heath, the Men's Pond stayed open. However, champion races and competitions were suspended.

By the early 1920s, the Men's Pond was again a popular bathing spot and it was then that the fathers of several of today's swimmers began to frequent the place. North London swimming clubs held their Club Championships at the pond, and sport was now becoming a matter of national pride. But the Men's Pond was also a place for fun. It was here that swimmers could take 'a seaside holiday in London'. Bathing outdoors was no longer something only to be taken for health purposes. 'It is indeed only lately that the hedonistic aspect of total immersion has eclipsed the therapeutic and that people go bathing not on the excuse that it is good for them, but frankly because they enjoy it,' declared *The Times*.

Swimming costumes had changed as well; they were no longer so utilitarian; instead they were becoming fashionable and available in an array of colours. For men the long one-piece affairs were replaced with shorter shorts and, while the torso was still covered, straps replaced sleeves. Women cast aside the wool jersey sleeveless tank suit, and instead wore newer, tighter fitting outfits made in dramatic stripes and bold patterns.

In 1922 the *Daily Express* described the Men's Pond as having 'pleasant graded slopes (on which one can enjoy a sun bath after the swim) surrounding the bathing pool. It is picturesque, fairly secluded, and large enough to accommodate several hundred swimmers and bathers. There are excellent diving rafts and stages, and the air of Parliament Hill is fresh and comparatively pure.' The idea of enjoying a 'sun bath' was relatively new. Originally sunbathing, much like bathing itself, was taken for health reasons. But by the 1920s it was becoming a leisurely pursuit, the bright young things of the French Riviera were eager to turn their white skins brown, and in the UK several groups were formed to extol the benefits of 'air bathing', including the Sunlight League and the Sun Bathing Society.

But while men may have sunbathed at the Men's Pond, the main draw continued to be swimming and diving, and in the 1920s and 30s women divers trained here in preparation for the Olympics. The image of the woman diver had by now become an international symbol, thanks to the Jantzen Knitting Company in the United States. It had begun producing bathing suits in 1910; known as Jantzens, and in 1920 introduced its Red Diving Girl logo on billboards, car stickers and on the suits themselves. This was the year that British diver Eileen Armstrong dived to glory when she won silver at the Olympics in Antwerp for high diving. London-born Armstrong was

No. 41-2. CAP
Made of pure worsted yarn. Jantzen rib stitch. Colors—Gray and green, black and gold, royal and white, green and white, gold and white, olive drab and emerald.

No. 225-SV. BATHING SUIT
Made of fine worsted yarn. Medium weight. Knit in the Jantzen elastic rib stitch, which fits the body at all times. Has small sleeve and border in neck. Colors—Same as cap. Sizes 34 to 44.

No. 537-2. BATHING SOX
Made of pure worsted yarn to match bathing suits. Medium weight. Elastic rib top and knit on hand machines. Colors—Same as cap. Sizes 8 to 11.

Below Bathing costumes started to become more fashionable and colourful; the Jantzen catalogue for 1918–1919 offered matching stockings and caps

No. 40-38. CAP

Made of pure worsted yarn. Light weight. Knit in the Jantzen elastic rib stitch. Made in colors to match your bathing suit—Scarlet and white, maroon and gold, green and white, copenhagen and gold.

No. 225-38. BATHING SUIT

Made of fine worsted yarn. Medium weight. Knit in the Jantzen elastic rib stitch. Colors—Scarlet and white, maroon and gold, green and white, copenhagen and gold. Sizes 34 to 44.

a member of the Mermaid Swimming Club, 'an elite club for ladies' formed in the 1890s, and according to local historian Rosalind Bayley she did some of her training at the Men's Pond.

In 1922 the old wooden diving stage was taken down, and replaced by a new concrete erection, as per the conditions required by the Amateur Diving Association and the Olympic Games Committee. The new structure was built to the north of the present day jetty, while the old one had lain to the south. The same year a springboard was put up, the first in the country. Three years later spectators were treated to the sight of seventy eight-year-old Sir Claude Champion de Crispigny and seventy one-year-old Otto Hagborg completing a stunning double dive. Sir Claude, a steeplechaser, balloonist and military adventurer, would later become president of the Amateur Diving Association.

Then, in 1928 the Highgate Diving Club, often described as the first professional British diving club, was formed at the Men's Pond and would dominate the national diving scene for decades to come. 'The history of diving in this country is incomplete without the Highgate Diving Club,' says club president McNally. 'It was an amateur club, but from 1928 to the present day there has always been a member in every Olympic Games, and that's a unequalled record.'

When Sandon wrote his brief history of the Men's Pond in 1923, he was evidently pleased that despite the low-key opening, it was now so well-known, and that membership of the Highgate Life-Buoys had risen to 110. He ends with the words 'I trust (the pond) will be a source of happiness and health to thousands upon thousands of people, both male and female, for many many years to come.' Sandon's wish came true, but he may not have imagined that two years later women would have a pond all of their own.

3. Kenwood Ladies' Bathing Pond

The Kenwood Ladies' Bathing Pond – or Highgate No.5 Pond – was opened to the public in 1926, although there had been calls for a women-only swimming spot for at least twenty years. In 1906, L. W. Balck of the Amateur Diving Association, and a life saving instructor at the Men's pond, had written to the press to complain about the Mixed and Men's ponds being closed between 11 a.m. and 2 p.m. This was 'particularly annoying to ladies' who could only use each pond one day a week, 'I am anxiously awaiting the realisation of my proposition that a pond at Highgate should be set apart entirely for ladies every day and all day from June to October on the same lines as the pond for men. The cost would be very small and the benefits incalculable.' But it took two decades until women got a pond to themselves, and this was a result of another major shift of ownership on Hampstead Heath.

The Ladies' Pond was one of the series of reservoirs that had been made in the late seventeenth century by the Hampstead Water Works Company, which had the lease on Millfield Farm. In 1789 the farm went on the market and the auction sale included 'Three Spacious Lakes, called the Highgate Ponds which supply Kentish Town and a great part of London with water.' The then owner of Kenwood House, William Murray, the 1st Earl of Mansfield, bought the farm and added it to his estate. Then in 1914 the 6th Earl of Mansfield decided to sell the estate – and the ponds – for building development. When World War I broke out, the plans were put on hold. But five years later he again considered selling the land and such were the rumours over what would happen that

questions were raised in the House of Commons. The Kenwood Preservation Council was hurriedly set up, it issued an appeal for funds and raised enough to buy around 100 acres, which it then offered to the LCC, and in 1925 the land was opened to the public. Not long afterwards, Kenwood House became public property as well, after its owner Edward Cecil Guinness, the 1st Earl of Iveagh, bequeathed it in his will.

However, people had bathed in the Ladies' Pond long before the official opening, when in theory only Lord Mansfield's friends and family could use it. At one stage it was leased to Highgate School, in 1914 a temporary high diving stage was erected, and after the war Lord Mansfield sometimes allowed boy scouts to swim there.

Women also used the pond before it was handed to the public. Irmgard Schaeffer was taken there by two German friends in the early 1920s, 'Our pond was then and for a long time afterwards very private. A grass path led to a wooden plank with a couple of primitive huts for changing and a bench for clothes. There were a few moorfowl, plenty of pike and small fry which used to terrify the women when they swam down their cleavages.' The pond would never lose this sense of being private and somewhat exclusive, but now, at last, all women would be able to use it.

On 9 June 1926 *The Times* reported, 'No. 5 Highgate Pond, one of the string of ponds lying under the slopes of Highgate, and until lately enclosed in private grounds, has been opened, as we recorded yesterday, to the feminine portion of the bathing public. The news will be welcome to the nymphs of north London.' The paper suggested that the pond could become a pleasant place, once trees and flowering shrubs were planted, although the waters were 'a little turbid on account of the soil.' But *The Times* realized the importance of the pond to a new breed of competitive women swimmers; 'it may be confidently expected that No. 5 Highgate will in due time train its champions, as champions in other sports are trained, somehow or another, in London. Swimming on the scale on which it is now practiced is curiously modern, even among men and boys, to say nothing of girls and women.' Indeed women would initially swim in the Ladies' Pond and bystanders would flock to watch them. Hours were generous during the summer, from 6.30 a.m. to 9 p.m. three days a week, and the journey could be made by five LCC Tramway services – from Holborn and Moorgate – at a cost of tuppence.

The LCC set to work improving facilities, installing a new wooden shed for changing, with a handful of cubicles for hire, while a small area of meadow was set aside

Left Dorothy May, daughter of boatman Walter May, worked at the Ladies' Pond in the 1920s. A martial arts expert and member of two swimming clubs, she hand-knitted the swimmers' costumes herself

for sunbathing. It also erected two competition height boards, a 1m springboard and a 3m flat rigid board, and two diving platforms. The LCC Parks Department then drew up a list of rules. There would be women lifeguards only, unless the qualified woman lifeguard was not on duty, in which case a qualified male attendant could step in. It also decided 'not to accede to a request' that mixed bathing be allowed. Its minutes don't state who this request came from, but the pond was thus saved for women only – although they were still allowed to use the men's pond on Wednesdays after 5 p.m.

The first recorded attendant at the Ladies' Pond was Lillian King, known as 'Kingy', whose husband was the Head Keeper. She opened the pond each day for the next twenty years, cycling from her home in Hornsey. King ensured swimmers were properly attired, with 'full costumes practically to the knees', and women had to prove they could swim by making it successfully to the second lifebuoy. Kingy was said to be strict with the swimmers, but always kind, and once rescued a woman who told her, 'Thank you, thank you for saving me. I was just married.'

One early morning swimmer, Margaret Vanek, says she never saw Kingy enjoy swimming for its own sake, but once saw her dive in and swim with a powerful stroke to rescue a woman in difficulties. Vanek would show the sort of commitment to the pond that many would emulate in the years to come. As a teenager she would skip breakfast, 'much to the annoyance of my father', and at 7 a.m. would rush to the Ladies' Pond, sometimes playing truant from school. Once, while climbing over the back gate before opening time, her shoes got stuck between the spikes. She even swam in January, 'The first dive took my breath away, but the exhilaration of those waters enticed me to become an all-year swimmer.'

But while King was apparently the first attendant, Dorothy May, daughter of Men's Pond boatman Walter May, also worked at the Ladies' Pond in the early years. Born in 1900, Dorothy was the only daughter among seven boys, two of whom were bare-knuckle fighters. A black belt martial arts and judo expert, she was a member of two swimming clubs and used to knit the swimmers' costumes herself. 'My grandmother was the keeper of the Ladies' Pond, although she was a bit cagey about her time there and we're unsure about her exact involvement,' says John Neal, 'But we used to look at photographs of her at the pond when we were kids. There's a picture of my Nan looking at a woman coming out of the water all covered in grease, because she was training for a Channel swim.'

Right Onlookers flocked to the Ladies' Pond to watch the swimmers

Ladies Swimming Pond, Highgate.

It wasn't long before a club was formed at the Ladies' Pond. Members of the Kenwood Regulars met every Saturday and Sunday, often breaking the ice in order to swim. The *Ham & High* reported: 'Plenty of swimming and no coddling is the advice of a score of young office girls to keep free from 'flu and other winter ills. These are the members of the Kenwood Regulars Swimming Club ... some of them come all the way from Kensington and Westminster.' On this occasion, in April 1927, twelve 'girls' wearing hand-knitted costumes of brightly coloured wool, were competing for a silver challenge cup in a 50 yards handicap race. The club's secretary, Miss Laura Toplis, told the press, 'Some of the girls hope to attempt the Channel some day.' This was not as unlikely as it once might have seemed, for the summer before nineteen-year-old American Gertrude Ederle had become the first woman – and the fastest person ever – to swim the Channel, knocking more than two hours from the previous record.

The media was fascinated by female swimmers, especially those who swam in winter, and *Pathé News* made at least two films at the Ladies' Pond. One, made on 29 December 1927, entitled 'Lady All The Year Round Swimmers', covers an annual holiday handicap race. A handful of women, in simple costumes and some with bathing caps, dive in to the pond on what looks like a freezing day, rain lashing down. They swim furiously to a wooden barrier and back, except for one who apparently gets into difficulties and is pulled out by two men on a boat.

The women were probably members of the Kenwood Regulars, which were now allowed to use the lifeguard's hut to store a stove and make tea, and which held well-attended galas at the pond in 1928 and 1929. Another Pathé clip shows around twenty swimmers jogging down the pathway where a woman, dressed in a full length Macintosh belted firmly at the waist, pulls a thermometer out of the water. The air is 1°C, the water nearly 4°C. The women wave at the camera and then dive in, watched avidly by spectators from the opposite bank. These, the film reminds us, are 'Modern Spartans!'

In 1929 the LCC decided that open-air bathing would remain free at the Ladies' Pond, suggesting that there had been moves to introduce charges. It also adopted some new rules; no dogs were to be allowed, although they could be tied up inside the outer fence. Sunbathing would be allowed 'only at times when, in the opinion of the officer in charge, inconvenience is not likely to result'. Bathers had to wear costumes or slips, as 'in the past many persons have sunbathed in a nude state.'

The meadow within the pond's boundaries had by now expanded, mainly because women wouldn't

With *Pathé News*, local and national press, the women at the Ladies' Pond soon became accustomed to publicity

Top left The Kenwood Regulars held well-attended galas in the late 1920s and were allowed to use the lifeguards' hut to store tea-making equipment
Bottom left Swimmers hold an impromptu boxing match at the Ladies' Pond; some are members of a rival group, the Excelsior Swimming Club
Below Regulars sitting on the springboard

keep to the small fenced off area they had been given, and it was here that 'some German émigrés' sunbathed nude. Sunbathing was now widely regarded as having serious health benefits. In 1932 writers and campaigners including Dora Russell, Vera Brittain, George Bernard Shaw and C.E.M. Joad wrote to *The Times*. 'Sir, – It is becoming increasingly manifest to the observant that this nation is rapidly awakening to the fact that so-called "sutu bathing", or to be more correct "active air bathing", is extremely beneficial to the health and happiness of the indoor worker.' But what to wear – or not to wear – for sunbathing was problematic. In April 1934 the LCC turned down an application that 'facilities for exercising and sunbathing without clothing' be provided at the Ladies' Pond. But this didn't deter those who wanted to take their clothes off, and visitors to the pond in the 1930s remember plenty of naked women.

Yet despite the pond's popularity in the early years, the number of early morning swimmers began to drop. In 1930 the *Ham & High* reported that unless an average of twenty women swam a day then the LCC would put a stop to morning swimming on weekdays altogether. However it was suggested that 'the winter has been too mild for (swimmers) to desire to exhibit their female hardihood.'

Perhaps women just didn't like the state of the water. One swimmer at the time, Mary Lawton, remembered the pond as 'a nice clean pond to swim in' but not everyone liked the mud. The water was 'rather green' and water snails were 'dumped in to clean the water', which led to worries among swimmers that their toes would be nibbled. But other reports refer to the water as being 'very dense and black', as it was in the early 1930s when the body of a twenty-year-old probationer nurse was pulled from the pond.

In the summer of 1930, when the Kenwood Regulars held their third annual gala at the pond, women were seriously outnumbered. All the competition winners were men, except for the winner of the senior obstacle race. The following year no gala was held. Another club was formed in 1932, the Kenwood Kingfishers' Swimming Club whose thirty five members swam throughout the year, but it didn't last very long. The pond was seldom crowded, even at weekends, and at its busiest only around fifty women swam. Just six years after opening, the future of the Kenwood Ladies' Bathing Pond appeared to hang in the balance.

Swimmers enjoying the Ladies'
Pond in all weathers during the
1920s. Their love of winter bathing
meant the media dubbed them
'Modern Spartans'

4.
The Ponds
in the 1930s

Life at the Mixed and the Men's Ponds in the 1930s was as busy as ever. The Mixed Pond now had a new amateur swimming group, the Hampstead Heath Swimming Club, formed in 1919 after the demise of an earlier club, the Water Rats, which had wound up sometime after the war. Members (men only) met every Sunday morning, often sons and fathers from the same family, and five trophy events were introduced, including the Mr Reed Trophy. 'It was the most beautiful piece of silverwork,' remembers Tony Duthie, 'when my father Frank won it my mother was so frightened it would be stolen that she wrapped it up in an old towel and hid it in a galvanized tub with the rest of the dirty wash whenever they were going out.' The Hampstead men also swam an annual race against the Serpentine Swimming Club, beginning in 1923, and when this was cancelled ten years later, the race was held from then on against the Highgate Life-Buoys.

Over at the Highgate Men's Pond, diving continued to be a major draw. Crowds still gathered to watch gala events, while men (and sometimes women) continued to train for Channel swims. A 'water swing' was installed in 1933 – 'the

HAMPSTEAD
for the Heights o' London

Cheap Day
Return Fare **8**D From this
Station

For availability and conditions of issue see hand-
bills obtainable at Booking Office

weight of the bathers carries it backwards and forwards, and falls are not dangerous in the least' reported the *Daily Mirror* – while a summer aquatic carnival drew crowds of 10,000 people. In 1929 a 100-yard handicap race was held for married men versus single. The marrieds lost. The same year boatman Walter May retired after thirty three years of service. 'We very much regret to lose an old friend. He did his job well and tactfully,' said C.A. Rosen, honorary secretary of the Life-Buoys. Contributions were asked for, a tidy sum of £66 was collected, and a presentation was made on Christmas morning, with a speech by Alister MacDonald, son of Prime Minister Ramsay MacDonald.

In 1930, in an attempt to improve safety, the LCC sloped the bank, and turfed and enclosed it with an iron fence. But conditions were still regarded as dangerous. On a Bank Holiday evening on 1 August 1938, a twenty four-year-old man, said to be a healthy, muscular, prize winning swimmer, disappeared while swimming to the raft and his body was eventually recovered in 14ft of water. 'Anybody who gets into difficulty in this pond where it is dark is beyond help, and it is merely a fluke if he can be got at,' said the St Pancras Coroner, 'If he goes below the surface, nobody can discover him at all because the water is dark and murky. This adds risk to the pond that some people may not realise.' The year before, the coroner had called the Hampstead Heath ponds 'death traps.' But the *St Pancras Gazette* noted that while there had been 'several fatalities', considering the large number of bathers the figure was comparatively small. It wondered whether 'some bathers over state their powers of endurance.' In the 1930s at least a thousand lives were still being lost annually, reported the RLSS, because people remained unaware of the 'art of swimming'.

In the 1930s the Men's Pond became home to a new group of regulars; boxers and wrestlers whose interest wasn't so much the water but training in the enclosure. Percy Craske, who had his first swim on Good Friday 1932, later recalled, 'I'd been to the fair (and) I was watching people diving and swimming and I thought it's unbelievable, this is Good Friday, so early in the year. I came in and the enclosure was full of brown people boxing, lifting weights, doing exercises. I said, "Can I join?" "Yes, yes," said a nice old gentleman called Charlie Cox and he leant me a costume and I had a dip and that's been me from that day. We had bankers, ex-boxers, doctors, old chaps, train drivers, tram drivers, out of works and everybody knew each other, all different ranks but we were all the same level.' This was the height of the Great Depression and men brought supplies

Left An Underground Electric Railways Company Poster from 1930 advertising Hampstead Heath

and shared what they had with good-humoured banter. But they did stick to their political groups. 'On the right hand of the enclosure when you come in they was all Tories and when you turned on the left we were all the lefties, Communists, and working class. We used to sort of shout and jeer in a comical sort of way when someone came in who took umbrage (with us). We had a chap used to bring a big sack of the original Jewish bread from the East End, the black, and he'd come up with about six loaves in the sack every day and we'd sit down with our milk, and a bit of cheese, and we'd get sort of cries from the other end, you know, 'Don't choke yourself!' and all that.'

In the mid-30s, trainer Wally May began to take his protégés to the pond, after sessions at Jack Straw's Castle. May had started weight lifting as a boy in the gutters of London, before opening his own gym and then joining the army. He was discharged with two smashed knees, a bullet wound to the head and a bayonet wound in his left arm. But by 1939 he was throwing a 200lb weight about like a dumb-bell, and was known for having swum 'sixteen hours in fresh water', at the Men's Pond. May trained champion

Top left The Highgate Life-Buoys after the Christmas Day race at the Mixed Pond in 1933

Top right Swimmers line up at the Mixed Pond in the 1930s

Bottom right The Men's Pond diving board in 1930

Bathing Pond, Highgate. 103787.

boxer Len Harvey on the Heath, and also worked with 'Battling' Barbara Buttrick, who later founded the Women's International Boxing Federation.

But popular though the Mixed and the Men's Ponds were in the 1930s, there were still disputes over opening times and segregated swimming. In an angry letter to the *Ham & High*, C.E.M. Joad, a Men's Pond regular, mocked the 'prudish foibles' of the LCC for not allowing mixed bathing, 'On Tuesday and Thursday when the Highgate Pond has been so uncomfortably full that queues have had to line up to await their turn, not more than a score of women have been enjoying the comparative solitude of Hampstead. So extreme is the terror of the LCC of an overlap between the sexes that no man may enter the Hampstead enclosure for a bathe after 8 a.m., though no woman may approach it before 9 a.m., with the result that many business people are unable to get a bathe before their day's work. ...The proximity of men and women in the process of uncovering their bodies, which unfortunately is a necessary preliminary of immersion is felt to create so alarming a situation that ... it must at all costs be prevented. Although it is considered decent for me to bathe with my daughter at Hornsey or Hammersmith, I may not do so a few miles away at Hampstead.' But in 1938 those like Joad who wanted to swim with their children, or men and women who wanted to swim together, would be able to. For now there would be a new place to swim on Hampstead Heath, the Parliament Hill Lido.

Snapshots from John Neal's family album reflecting life at the Men's Pond where his great grandfather Walter May was boatman

Top The prize giving for the annual round the pond race held every May in the 1950s
Bottom May's daughter Dorothy sitting in the bow of her father's boat in 1908

Bottom Christmas morning, 1919

Bottom May with one of his sons, Lovey, in the 1920s

Centre May with his children and wife Hannah, circa 1908

Bottom Sonny May (centre), one of Walter's younger sons, and friends, circa 1920

Top The wooden diving platform in the 1920s

Bottom Walter May held aloft, circa 1950

5.
The Parliment Hill Lido

The Parliament Hill Lido – also known as the Gospel Oak Lido – was built during the golden age of lido construction, as part of a government drive to improve the nation's health, and especially that of the working class. The aim was to produce a fitter nation with a far better 'National Physique' – and what better to build than outdoor pools? Between 1930–39, at least 180 lidos were built in Britain, adding to the fifty built the decade before. And it was the LCC that led the way. 'I promised the people of London that the new LCC would make London a "City of Lidos". Here we are,' announced Herbert Morrison in the summer of 1937. Morrison, then leader of the LCC, which had come under Labour control three years earlier, would later become Labour deputy prime minster.

Suddenly there was a surge in construction; the Physical Training and Recreation Act allowed borough councils to apply for grants to hire the unemployed, and the LCC promised that soon no Londoner would have to travel more than one and a half miles to enjoy open-air swimming. The new pools would be places where people could deliberately set out to enjoy their leisure time, and as a result of the Annual Holiday Bill of 1936, employees now had paid holidays for the first time.

But one of the biggest draws of the lido was the notion that men and women could swim together. Mixed bathing had already been introduced at the Serpentine or Hyde Park Lido, the first to be built in London, with huge success. On opening day in 1930 hordes ran out of a large tent marked 'WOMEN', eager to mingle with the men at the poolside. Together they dived in, cheering and waving to the cameras, a bobbing mass of men, women and children.

But what exactly was a lido? The term comes from the Latin word *litus*, meaning shore or coastline. The original lido is the thin stretch of sandy island that encloses the lagoon of Venice – the Lido di Venezia. Here people bathed in the sea from the late nineteenth century, and the resort became known as simply 'the lido'. The term also gave rise to the 'lido deck' on a cruise ship.

Purpose built open-air pools weren't new, but in the 1920s and 30s the lido became a staple of many European city parks. In the UK, some popular seaside resorts had already built their own open-air pools – Scarborough in 1915 and Blackpool in 1923. While these weren't called lidos, they did have sunbathing terraces, cafés, and areas for spectators, all important features of lido life.

But there was a certain amount of snobbery attached to the term 'lido'. An editorial in *The Times*, referring to the Ruislip Lido, decried the notion of 'calling a suburban reservoir … after an Adriatic beach patronised by wealthy cosmopolitans. Lidos are still new and parvenus and jarring, an insult to our taste and to our self-respect. Behind the pert misnomer yawns an abyss of snobbery.' Snobbery also came into play in terms of pronunciation. 'My first encounter with English class distinctions occurred when pronouncing the word "Lido",' recalls one user of the Ruislip Lido. 'My parents, who had pretensions of upper mobility, insisted that it should be pronounced "Leedo" while my school friends cheerfully said "Lyedo".' At Parliament Hill, most local children called it 'Lyedo' too. However it was pronounced, by 1937 the LCC had come up with a definition of a lido; they were 'open-air swimming baths with the added amenities of sun-bathing areas, cafés, and other facilities which will make them attractive places of healthy public

Left A stunning double dive performed at the opening of the Parliament Hill Lido

resort.' The baths would have 'fine proportions, cheerful colours, convenient dressing accommodation', as well as flowerbeds and a vista of trees. Lido pools tended to be rectangular and were often Olympic-sized, with shallow and deep ends, and an array of diving and spring boards. At one end was the engine house, which pumped clean water through the pool, while at the other end were often ornamental fountains, which aerated the water. There were changing rooms and places to buy food and drink; some lidos had dancing facilities; others had underwater lighting or were floodlit at night with coloured bulbs. There was normally a wall enclosing the whole lido, to keep people from getting in without paying and to act as a suntrap and windbreak. After all, the lidos were open to the skies; they and their swimmers were part of nature. Architecturally, many took their inspiration from the cruise liner; even the railings around a lido café looked like the railings of a ship's deck. Here was an example not just of fine engineering, but of art. The Jubilee Pool in Penzance for example, which opened in 1935, was reportedly built to resemble a seagull landing on water.

Life around the pool was an important part of lido life; this was a place to see and be seen. Members of the Women's League of Health and Beauty, formed in 1930 by Mary Bagot Stack, held keep-fit displays, while others paraded in poolside beauty pageants. Images of women in fashionable skin-tight bathing suits were everywhere, on railway posters and the covers of magazines, in adverts for cigarettes, cars and soft drinks. The Jantzen Company in the States used movie stars like Ginger Rogers to promote their suits and their magazine adverts showed bronzed men admiring women wearing 'America's finest fitted swimming suit'. 'Skip the flattery, darling,' declares one bathing beauty, 'My Jantzen takes care of that.' But the average costume for men and women remained remarkably similar and both often wore a two-piece with a belt. Men's torsos were still covered, as they still had to be on most beaches, but women's costumes sometimes had decorative holes cut at the sides – all the better for catching a tan. Towards the end of the 30s the two-piece, resembling a

Images of women in fashionable bathing suits were everywhere in the 1930s; a Jantzen advert from a 1935 edition of *Tatler* (below), and a Harrods catalogue from 1938 (right)

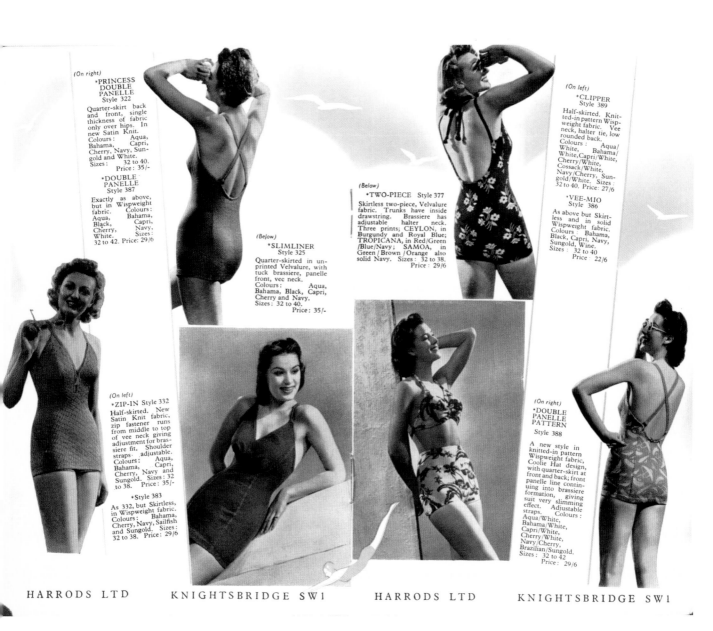

(On right)
*PRINCESS DOUBLE PANELLE
Style 322

Quarter-skirt back and front, single thickness of fabric only over hips. In new Satin Knit. Colours: Aqua, Bahama, Capri, Cherry, Navy, Sungold and White. Sizes: 32 to 40. Price: 35/-

*DOUBLE PANELLE
Style 387

Exactly as above, but in Wispweight fabric. Colours: Aqua, Bahama, Capri, Black, Cherry, Navy, White. Sizes: 32 to 42. Price: 29/6

(Below)
*SLIMLINER
Style 325

Quarter-skirted in un-printed Velvalure, with tuck brassiere, panelle front, vee neck. Colours: Aqua, Bahama, Black, Capri, Cherry and Navy. Sizes: 32 to 40.
Price: 35/-

(Below)
*TWO-PIECE Style 377

Skirtless two-piece, Velvalure fabric. Trunks have inside drawstring. Brassiere has adjustable halter neck. Three prints; CEYLON, in Burgundy and Royal Blue; TROPICANA, in Red/Green /Blue/Navy; SAMOA, in Green/Brown/Orange also solid Navy. Sizes: 32 to 38.
Price: 29/6

(On left)
*CLIPPER
Style 389

Half-skirted. Knit-ted-in pattern Wisp-weight fabric. Vee neck, halter tie, low rounded back. Colours: Aqua/White, Bahama/White, Capri/White, Cherry/White, Cossack/White, Navy/Cherry, Sun-gold/White. Sizes: 32 to 40. Price: 27/6

*VEE-MIO
Style 386

As above but Skirt-less and in solid Wispweight fabric. Colours: Bahama, Black, Capri, Navy, Sungold, Wine. Sizes: 32 to 40
Price: 22/6

(On left)
*ZIP-IN Style 332

Half-skirted. New Satin Knit fabric, zip fastener runs from middle to top of vee neck giving adjustment for bras-siere fit. Shoulder straps adjustable. Colours: Aqua, Bahama, Capri, Cherry, Navy and Sungold. Sizes: 32 to 38. Price: 35/-

*Style 383

As 332, but Skirtless, in Wispweight fabric. Colours: Bahama, Cherry, Navy, Sailfish and Sungold. Sizes: 32 to 38. Price: 29/6

(On right)
*DOUBLE PANELLE PATTERN
Style 388

A new style in knitted-in pattern Wispweight fabric, Coolie Hat design, with quarter-skirt at front and back; front panelle line contin-uing into brassiere formation, giving suit very slimming effect. Adjustable straps. Colours: Aqua/White, Bahama/White, Capri/White, Cherry/White, Navy/Cherry, Brazilian/Sungold. Sizes: 32 to 42
Price: 29/6

HARRODS LTD   KNIGHTSBRIDGE SW1   HARRODS LTD   KNIGHTSBRIDGE SW1

bikini, was already in evidence, although it would be another ten years before this was officially named and launched.

Aside from poolside displays, a major attraction of lido life was the new range of diving opportunities. The cult of diving reached its height in the 1930s, helped by *Olympia*, the prize-winning film of the 1936 summer Olympics that featured breathtaking diving displays. According to Ken Worpole, 'The art of diving, and the photographic iconography of the arched body of the diver in mid-flight belongs … to the lido.' Diving was not just a sporting achievement but, as with displays at the Highgate Men's Pond, a theatrical experience.

By the mid 1930s the exotic word lido had been widely adopted, at least in the popular sense. 'Lido has added a new word to our language and a new recreation to our habits,' intoned a *Pathé News* reporter. It was where 'all and sundry take the waters and the sun … now you see why lido has supplanted Ludo.' So when the people of Hampstead and St Pancras heard that a new lido would be built at Parliament Hill there

was plenty of interest, and unlike the three bathing ponds on the Heath, its opening was well documented. In the summer of 1937, as part of its plan for a 'City of Lidos', the LCC submitted proposals for a chain of five open-air swimming pools, with the Parliament Hill Lido situated on 2.5 acres of land once known as the Salisbury Plain. It was designed by two LCC architects, Harry Rowbotham and T.L. Smithson, who designed all thirteen of the LCC's lidos built between 1906 and 1939. While the chosen site was on 'a secluded part of the Heath' according to *The Times*, the pool was expected to attract 200,000 people. The press kept people fully informed about construction plans. Readers were repeatedly told the size of the pool – 200ft by 90ft – and its capacity, 650,000 gallons of water. There would be separate swimming hours for men and women and, most daringly, set hours for mixed swimming as well. The pool would be open every day during the summer, when for five days a week men and boys could swim for free in the early mornings. On the remaining two days it was the turn of girls and women. The lido would also open for mixed bathing from 10 a.m. to closing time on four days a week and bank holidays, at a charge of sixpence. However not everything went to plan; a glazier's strike delayed the official opening and while the pool was full of water by 30 July 1938, the windows had no glass. But the strike ended and the lido opened a few weeks later, at an eventual cost of £34,000. The building included a main entrance facing Gordon House Road, with a separate entrance for spectators on the northwest side, which led to two spectators' terraces, with steps for sunbathing. The poolside was paved with buff, handmade, pre-cast paving slabs, while the pool was lined with blue glazed brickwork. Swimmers had to walk through wading pools before getting into the water, which was 2ft 6ins at the shallow end and 9ft 6ins at the deep end. There were 3m fixed and spring diving boards, a 5m diving board, an ordinary springboard, as well as two chutes. Capacity was 2,000 bathers, with 178 cubicles and 1,072 lockers.

The raised terrace around the pool was built as if for people to watch a performance. And on opening day on Saturday 20 August 1938 there was quite a show – although the oft-repeated assertion that American film stars Tyrone Power and Victor Mature were present is a myth. 500 people packed the poolside as the Secretary of the Football Association, Stanley Rous, gave the opening address. He seemed a little confused as to why he'd been invited, saying he could see no connection between football and swimming, but 'a great deal of money has been spent here and I for one feel that if 34,000 people learn to swim here in the next few years, it will have been money well spent.'

This was followed by a roll of drums by the Metropolitan Police Central Band and then a graceful double dive by Flying Officer C.D. Tomalin of the Highgate Diving Club and Miss J. Dixon of the Mermaid Swimming Club. The diving display also included 'an hilarious mock life saving episode,' according to the *Ham & High*. The Mayor of St Pancras, Councillor John Sperni, thanked the aquatic generosity of the LCC, while an LCC representative said it was about time the very poor had access to the sort of facilities normally only available to the very rich. The ceremony over, the crowds waiting outside were finally allowed to enter; the doors opened and in they trooped cheering. No mention is made of any lifeguards in the press reports, and the lido was probably run by a park keeper; a white-coated individual who dealt with the machinery and who was unlikely to have known how to swim. But two 'Keep-Fit' instructors were present on certain days, with free 'advice and hints' on swimming, diving and life saving.

Yet while the lido opened with great fanfare, World War II was already on the horizon. The press had announced air raid precautions, the first million civilian volunteers had enrolled, shelters were being erected and plans made for the possible evacuation of children. It was also suggested that a first aid post be set up at the lido, which had its own ambulance room, although this was later abandoned. Even before the lido opened, people were filling sand bags from the construction debris. 'They had dug up where the pool would be,' remembers Paul Thorogood, 'and extracted soil to dig a hole, and there was a great heap of it near the railway line. People filled bags with sand or whatever it was. I was about seven years old and someone chucked a brick at me and I still have the scar today.' Thorogood went to the lido as soon as it opened and it was there that he learned to swim, later getting a job in the basket area and winning medals in the North London LCC championships.

During the long hot summer of 1939, London lidos still swarmed with life. But when war was declared in September, one by one the nation's lidos began to close. The Parliament Hill Lido took a direct hit during the Blitz when, on 13 September 1940, incendiary bombs caused seventeen local fires. The last fell on the lido at 10.13 p.m., but the fire brigade managed to extinguish each blaze within twenty minutes, and the lido remained open. This was much to the relief of local children. 'In the summer of 1943 I visited the lido most days,' recalls Roy Naisbitt, 'I was thirteen and I remember how lively it was, full of children and families. I don't remember people ever swimming up and down or across the pool, just a mass of people going in all directions, splashing around and enjoying themselves.'

When war ended in 1945, life remained hard for most people, the country was poor and food and clothes were still rationed. Few households had televisions or cars, and lidos became urban resorts for post-war babies. Leeroy Murray remembers his first visit to the Parliament Hill Lido in 1948 when he was three years old. 'I sat down at the shallow end and I looked at the vast body of water that seemed to go on forever, it was a whole world. And then gingerly I got in.' Murray lived in a prefab, next to a bombsite where Gospel Oak Primary School now stands, and the lido quickly became a way of life. 'We experienced the deprivations of most post-war families. Luckily we had Hampstead Heath, and the lido was our saving grace.'

6. The Ponds in War and Beyond

As with the lido, the bathing ponds also stayed open during World War II, although in the early days it had looked like they would close. In 1936 the Metropolitan Water Board, created to merge the companies that supplied water to London, had decided not to renew its lease on the springs that fed the ponds. Railway companies had stopped using the water from the Hampstead and Highgate Ponds, which ended up at a reservoir on Camden Park Road, and the Board grew worried about cost, especially as it still had to pay an annual rent charge. Although it decided not to renew its lease with the City of London Corporation, it suggested a tablet be erected to 'record the antiquity of the ponds' as a source of water supply. This was never done. But when the Corporation considered draining the ponds, the press reported that the LCC would keep them open for the time being.

Despite the war, Hampstead Heath was still a popular place to go. *Pathé News* described it as a resort for 'stay at home London holiday makers (with) forests and woodlands and a natural lake that makes swimming a pleasure and diving a thrill … If you ken Kenwood, girls, you'll take your prettiest bathing suit and give it an airing either in the water or on the water's edge. With a little amount of imagination, Vera, you might be on the Riviera.'

But the fencing at many of the ponds suffered badly during the war. The Hampstead Heath and Old Hampstead Protection Society reported that at the Men's Pond iron fencing had been removed from the south side, while at the Mixed Pond 'as fast as the wooden fence is repaired it is smashed and fresh openings are made'. Unlike the Parliament Hill Lido however, none of the bathing ponds were directly hit during the war, although a handful of high explosives and incendiaries fell near the Mixed Pond, and in the summer of 1944 the fifth doodlebug or flying bomb to fall on Hampstead landed on its bank.

Left The bathing ponds stayed open during the war; swimmers brave the waters at the Mixed Pond, circa 1942

The Mixed Pond

Despite earlier promises that bathing would remain free, it was during the war that the Mixed Pond became the first pond where swimmers had to pay. The LCC introduced charges of six pence for children and one shilling for adults, although swimming was still free before 10 a.m. By now men and women were swimming together, just as they were at the lido. In the summer the raft was crowded, divers made use of the fixed boards and springboard, while others lay along the banks sunbathing. 'We went to the Mixed Pond a lot because we were young and wanted to be mixed,' says Margaret Hepburn, who moved to London in her twenties. 'It was a funny time after the war, people were coming out of the forces and a lot of people were quite lost. It was very comforting going to the Mixed Pond.' She remembers holding a party at the pond following the Hampstead Arts Ball (modelled on the Chelsea Arts Club fancy dress balls held at the Albert Hall), 'We took the gramophone onto the raft, but how we got it there I have no idea.'

The Hampstead Heath Swimming Club, which hadn't met for ten years, resumed its activities after the war and quickly reinstated the traditional Christmas Day race, a 25-yard swim to three posts in the water at the shallow end and back. 'If you were lucky you could turn at the post and use it to kick off from,' recalls Tony Duthie, 'if you were unlucky then you touched the rope and felt the mud underneath.' Duthie joined the club in 1949 when, at the age of fifteen, he won the Christmas Day race. The starter was Claude Lusty, club president and licensee of the Magdala Tavern. Duthie recalls his day of triumph, 'Lusty started the race off, which was handicapped, and he gave a slow count. Possibly he was inexperienced in counting the swimmers off, or he'd had a little too much the night before, but by the time he got to the count of ten he was already five seconds behind the stopwatch. Consequently the first three swimmers in the water came in 1st, 2nd, and 3rd.' Duthie's father, Frank, aged forty eight, came second, while A.H. Chipperfield – or 'Chip' – who worked as a chef for Crosse and Blackwell, came third. 'He always came third,' says Duthie, 'and there was no trophy for third so he gave himself one.' Chip was club treasurer and vice president and today there is a bench in his memory at the Mixed Pond.

The race – as with the club as a whole – was still for boys and men only, and spectators were mainly members, friends and relatives. Often conditions were freezing and the ice had to be broken first. The pond's LCC keeper would go out on the boat and hit the ice with the oars to make a space to swim, then hand his hat round afterwards

Below Boxing in the men's changing area at the Mixed Pond, 1948

Top right Tony Duthie (centre) won the 1949 Christmas Day race at the age of fifteen

Bottom right Swimmers exercising at the Mixed Pond, 1948

for donations. Duthie remembers one Christmas morning, as soon as the ice was broken it started forming again and when the swimmers got out they had cuts all over their bodies. The club also produced a Christmas card showing a figure about to dive off the board, which was covered in icicles. 'That,' says Duthie, 'was my father.'

Several new trophies were introduced in the 1950s; including the Austin Memorial Trophy for the member with the highest aggregate number of points. Members could gain points in a variety of ways, two for attendance at the pond before 9.30 a.m. in winter and one if they came before 9 a.m. the rest of the year. There were also points for doing well in a race. 'I was around twelve when I was persuaded to go into the pond by my father Ken, although I didn't want to,' remembers Clive Stewart, 'We got there and I dived in, swam 25 yards across the pond and 25 yards back and got out. "Well done", my father said, "you got three points".* The Stewart family can be seen in a 1951 BBC film of the Christmas Day race. Clive's brother Robin, aged around eleven, is one of the first to leap in, wearing trunks made by his mother Kitty, who stands on the bank cheering them on.

The Hampstead Club continued to race against the Highgate Life-Buoys and in one memorable year, 1956, they actually won – by a fifth of a second. The press reported, 'An excellent swim with a well judged last few yards spurt by the Hampstead Heath captain K. Stewart, and a superb effort by Life-Buoys last man, F. Waters who had traveled all night by train from Bradford.'

The Highgate Men's Pond

At the outbreak of war the Highgate Life-Buoys had an impressive 250 members. When the younger men were called into service, the older ones carried on, although championship races and other events were suspended. Some of today's swimmers remember conscientious objectors and deserters 'hanging around the pond' in wartime. Every now and again there was a police raid, which sometimes meant a quick dive into the water. 'The pond became a refuge for people who refused to go to war,' says one regular, 'they had witnessed what had happened in the First World War, and they remained on the run or were jailed. However, some men volunteered to fight the first day, and these seemingly diametrically opposed groups remained true friends until they died.'

In the post war years the pond continued to attract divers, winter bathers and sportsmen, as well as a new breed of iron men. 'The pond was like a health club,' remembers former stuntman Peter Brace, 'everyone was training. It was all the lads who were out of work. There was a keeper called Alf, who was 6ft 4ins and wore big boots, and a postman with tattoos down his arms who would swim 100m and back and just shake himself off. Then there were the regulars like Harold the Ogre and Doc Bruise, a hairy apple of a man who would bend down and say a prayer and it took for ages before he dived in.'

Brace found jumping off the 10m board useful practice for his work in films such as Batman and TV shows like the New Avengers. 'It was very handy for getting used to the feel of going through the air. It was quite painful; hitting the water even feet first you got a right slap. The Highgate Diving Club would do displays and they'd come out afterwards with twisted arms and shoulders and covered in bruises. Some of them got quite punch drunk. Water is hard; even if you do it right it's a hard blow. But nobody worried about health and safety then.'

'Long-time Dave' can attest to that. He first came across the Men's Pond in 1939, when he wasn't allowed in because he couldn't swim. But he returned after the war and became a regular. 'I remember a very windy sunny day when I was on the top diving board waiting for a lull in the wind. Then I dived, and I was caught by a gust of wind and I hit the water with a curved back. I ended up at the Whittington Hospital for a couple of weeks. It was like hitting a brick wall.' Many swimmers remember a man called Frank, who loved to dive at the Men's Pond. 'He had one leg with terrific muscle and a wooden leg and he had no bone in the elbow of one of his arms,' recalls one regular, 'He used to dive quite acrobatically off the top board.'

The media was still intrigued by winter swimmers, and often covered events at the Men's Pond. A small band of regulars included a clergyman, a doctor, several civil servants and a Fleet Street journalist who all had a pre-breakfast dip. 'All say they would sooner take a header into the pond than step gingerly into a cold bath,' reported *The Times*, 'Their only complaint is that they cannot satisfy the hearty appetite their swim has given them on present-day rations.' These winter bathers were certainly determined. On one foggy morning a man lost his sense of direction while out in the middle of the pond, until his friends guided him back 'by the means of electric torches.' Then there was the 'deeply religious' man who liked to dive from the top board. He would write out a prayer, which he carried down with him when 'visibility was such that he could not see the water or anything that might be on the surface.'

Bathers weren't put off by icy conditions either. In 1950, the race course first had to be cleared of ice and Life-Buoys president Thomas Robertson, who was then seventy two, didn't swim on doctor's orders, the first time he'd been unable to compete since the club was founded in 1903.

In December 1954 one enthusiast described his regular swim to the *Daily Express*. 'It was seven degrees below freezing point at 11.30 yesterday morning when I closed my front door on my way into Highgate Ponds, London.' He traveled by train until reaching the Heath, whereupon 'I walked over a mile through a gently swirling snow shower.' When he arrived at the pond five men had just been in, and an LCC keeper was using a wooden rake to keep a small area of water free from ice.

Two years later a *Times* correspondent joined a dozen hardened winter swimmers, 'An attendant of the London County Council had arrived at dawn to make a hole in the ice large enough to swim in. Drying in the sunshine afterwards, in spite of the low air temperature, was a comparatively pleasant experience. The swimmers found that the sudden shock of the immersion was quickly over and that afterwards they had a feeling of glowing warmth from head to toe.' The correspondent was clearly impressed by the regulars, 'An MP or two, lawyers, writers, actors, and one QC, as well as a Channel swimmer, are among those who make the journey from all parts of London each day to dive in Highgate pond in all weathers.' And conditions were certainly nippy, 'your Correspondent can vouch for the man who, on a cold morning this week, could not run his comb through his hair after his dip because he found it had frozen.' Later that year a member of the Life-Buoys known as 'Mahogany Cox' told the press that cold-water bathing was a recipe for an illness-free life. 'We rely on the icy champagne water,' he said, 'to give us the festive spirit.'

Left Bert Assirati 'the world's strongest man' doing neck exercises at the Men's Pond in 1936

Below Assirati poses with a featherweight Maclean bicycle, 1938

But the man most renowned for his ability to withstand cold water was a Life-Buoy named Harry Losner, also known as 'Goldfish' or 'Goldie'. 'He was unbelievable; there was no one like him,' says current Life-Buoys president Chris Ruocco, 'His party trick was to dive in under the springboard, swim out into the pond and then come up, breaking the ice with his hands. He would pop his head out and swim back. He used to swim up and down in the dark; he would do about a mile. But he did shiver when he came out.' Many swimmers say 'medical men' from the Medical Research Council laboratories at Holly Hill in Hampstead, took Goldie to the lab for research purposes where they poured cubes of ice on him to see how he could stand it. Today there is a bench in his memory on the lawn outside the pond.

Other pond lovers at the time included Labour politician Baron Eric Fletcher of Islington and industrialist Henry Kremer, a year-round swimmer who was driven to the pond by his chauffeur in the early morning.

In the 1950s the Men's Pond became even better known as a training venue for wrestlers, boxers, weightlifters, runners and gymnasts. Derek, a former weight trainer, remembers, 'In those days it was like a training camp. We came because it was free and people used to bring weights with them. A man called Mugabe was the best; we used to call him "The Hitman". He would say, "Good morning", and that was it, there was no conversation. But in the ring he was a killer.'

The 1950s were also a time of bodybuilding, when muscle men like Charles Atlas promised, 'I'll prove in seven days I can make you a new man!' Adverts for his training methods appeared in boys' comic books and images of bulging torsos were everywhere. British bodybuilder James Evans produced an illustrated manual which began with the words, 'Not many years ago anyone who possessed an outstanding physique and performed prodigious feats of strength was considered to be part and parcel of a travelling circus.' But now there was a new breed of men, 'who before the war never lifted their arms any higher than to rest them on top of their office desks.'

It was at the Men's Pond that wrestler Bert Assirati, once proclaimed the world's strongest man, used to train. A multiple British Heavyweight Champion, Assirati was known for being able to squat on one leg with a 200lb barbell on his shoulders; perform a backwards somersault while holding a 56lb block weight in each hand; and carrying a piano (or alternatively, a telegraph pole) over 'a long distance' on his back. 'I remember Bert

Assirati because nobody messed with him,' says one swimmer, 'He was short; around 5ft 8ins but he weighed twenty stone. He used to do hand stands on one hand in the enclosure. Once I was standing in the sun and I heard a voice, "You're in my sun". I was a cocky eighteen–year-old and I turned round and saw it was Bert. I was like, "right OK Bert!".'

'He was a remarkable character,' agrees Peter Brace, 'The men from the pond would play a sort of rugby on the grass outside on a Sunday morning, just throwing the ball round, there weren't really any rules. One day Bert ran down the slope to catch the ball, hit the fence and took down 20 yards. He wasn't bothered at all.'

Many boxers used the Men's Pond in the 50s, including Ruocco, who was then a ten-year-old member of the St Pancras Boxing Club. During the summer, under legendary trainer George Francis, the boys would run to the pond, jump in and run back. Ruocco liked it so much that, 'I used to go to school, get my marks and go straight to the pond.' Other boxers included lightweight champion Dave Crowley, and Sid Turner, sparring partner for Jack Dempsey, the American World Heavyweight Champion of the 1920s.

Many of the activities at the Men's Pond were deeply competitive. One swimmer remembers a kind of badminton played in the changing compound, with table tennis bats; 'It was taken very seriously by some, often leading to blows'. The pond was also home to water polo events, as well as deep-water divers. In 1957 members of the British Sub-Aqua Club – both men and women – were given permission to use the pond, an ideal place to train beginners in deep water during winter. While the water was far from clear, the pond was 'easy to reach, particularly during the petrol shortage,' reported *The Express*. 'Only my fingers are cold. I myself am quite warm,' Mayfair typist Lucia Giola told the paper as she stepped out of the pond in her black rubber diving suit. 'No water leaks through the suit's neckline,' she explained, 'And we wear ballet tights and sweaters underneath. The suit does not fit me properly because it was designed for a man'.

The depth of the Men's Pond also made it a perfect place to take the bronze life saving medal, which is what Paul Thorogood did before becoming a lifeguard. 'I never made a rescue there but I would tell people who were incompetent swimmers to get out. There were some eccentric and odd people. There was a Labour MP who would come in the early morning, tie his togs to the bar by the jetty, get in and swim. Then he got out, and walked along the jetty completely starkers. I told him off. He was very put out to be told off by a young whippersnapper like me.'

The Kenwood Ladies' Pond

At the Kenwood Ladies' Bathing Pond, lifeguard Lillian King was still in charge, 'in her white peaked cap like a ship's captain and little socks folded over her boots. It was her pond; she was the boss and she marched around saying, "Don't do this … or that".' Now that the Kenwood Regulars were no more, there were no competitive events, which meant the pond was out of the news. But earlier threats from the LCC to close the pond for early morning swimming had come to nothing, and it became a favoured place for nude swimming, as Barbara Dixon remembers.

She came to London in 1945 as a sixteen-year-old, from a small village in Lincolnshire, and worked at Bourne and Hollingsworth Department Store in Oxford Street. 'On Sunday mornings an older lady called Mary, a buyer in the bridal department, would suggest going to the Ladies' Pond. Mary was a little bit like that; she was a little bit offbeat. I went several times just after the war. I remember the pond had a big hedge around it. It wasn't a rough place and it was never crowded. I knew there was a Men's Pond too, because Mary pointed it out and then we got to our pond and she said, "It's only ladies here". But I never swam. And we were so horrified because women used to swim in the nude! They would rush out of the wooden changing rooms with a towel around them, take it off and jump in. We'd been brought up not to take our clothes off and we were horrified. The young girls from Bournes had quite a standard.'

Another visitor to the pond, Anthea Lonedes, remembers seeing a very famous figure. 'I went there in 1950 when I was around thirteen. There were women sunbathing with no clothes on and the brown wrinkled bodies of all these old women were like chestnuts. One day I saw Margaret Rutherford there. She was enormous. She went into the changing area, came out and turned around. She was like a battleship. She went down the steps to the pond, just down a few steps, and then she turned around and scooped the water up and splashed it on her face. Then she launched herself in and set off doing a strong breaststroke. She swam to the lifebelt at the far corner of the pond, stayed there a while and then swam back. And she did the entire thing naked. People didn't pay her much attention though, she must have gone to the pond quite often and people knew her.' Born in 1892, Rutherford later found fame as Miss Marple. In 1949 she had starred in the Ealing Studios comedy classic *Passport to Pimlico* and was about to start filming *The Magic Box* where her role was, suitably enough, Lady Pond.

7.
The Lido in the 1950s

In the 1950s the Parliament Hill Lido was still the favourite swimming spot for local children, especially during long hot summers. 'It was a community for us,' says Leeroy Murray, 'we would stay until we were so hungry we were forced to leave.' Children played on the slides, dived in and out of the fountain, sometimes clambering to the top, and then headed to the café for ice-lollies, hot Bovril and Eccles cakes. Many also found a way to get in without paying, and with spectator entrance and exit turnstiles on either side of the café, and exit turnstiles at each end of the terraces, the possibilities seemed endless. Lido users were supposed to pay to put their clothes in a basket, and were then given a rubber band to wear around the wrist. But children would climb over the wall and store their clothes wherever they could, piling their things near a couple so it would appear they were part of a family group. 'Guards, perhaps they were lifeguards, would walk around and say, "Where's your band for a basket?" Some patrolled, some turned a blind eye. I remember being told off, but I don't ever remember being chucked out.'

Supervision at lidos was still minimal, although volunteer lifesavers had been in place at the nation's beaches since the 1930s, when the RLSS had launched the Life Guard Corps to 'minimize the great loss of life which occurs annually during the bathing season.' Despite their name, they were life savers rather than lifeguards, using the lifeline method of rescue (consisting of a rope, harness and float), and in the 1950s women joined the ranks for the first time. But around 1,000 people still accidentally drowned each year in England and Wales during the holiday season, according to the Registrar General, and a quarter were children under fifteen. 'It is a paradox of our time that, while more and more youngsters are taught to swim, the art (or science) of life saving remains relatively a rare accomplishment', reported *The Times*. And while local authorities put up notices warning people not to go out of their depth, little else was done to ensure safety.

At lidos, revelers pretty much did as they wanted and there were few qualified people on hand to help in an emergency. The Serpentine Lido, billed as a major tourist attraction, drew as many as 9,000 bathers a day, yet there were only four 'guards' in boats. In the

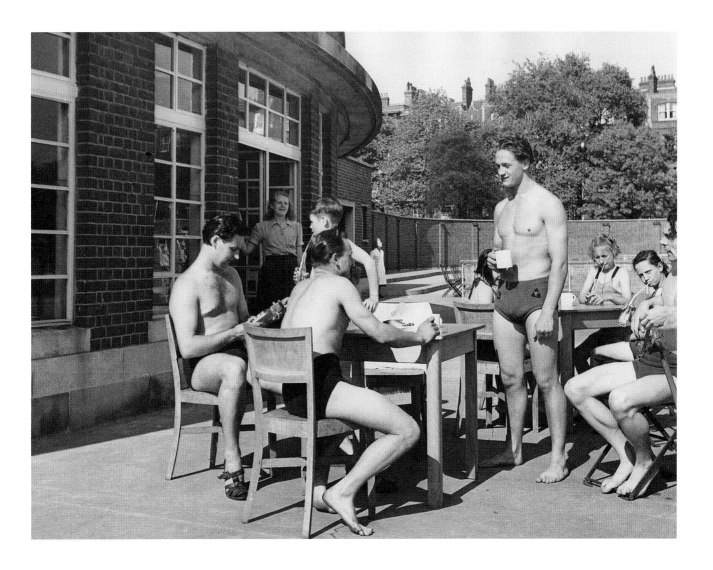

Above Swimmers relaxing outside
the lido's café in the mid 1950s

summer of 1957 a woman who had been swimming back to the bank found it impossible to get help when her fiancé disappeared. She told the coroner that when she'd approached a policeman, and eventually 'the first aid man', she had been laughed at.

At Parliament Hill Lido, children weren't asked about their swimming ability, nor were they barred from the deep end, and many jumped off diving boards when they could barely complete a width of the pool. Murray remembers climbing up the main diving tower 'and jumping off the boards like monkeys. People would be diving off the side springboard and they would spring so far they were in the tower area, where people were doing dive bombs. Once I was standing on the board ready to jump off. My brother Peter was in the water looking up and me and I said, "just stay there and I'll jump just beside you, I won't land on you." He waited and I jumped on top of his head. He never forgave me for that.'

The only real health and safety fears related to the spread of the highly infectious poliovirus, a frequent cause of death and paralysis, especially among children, until a vaccine was introduced in 1955. Initially it was thought that stagnant water spread the disease, and children were warned to stay away from ponds or areas of still water during hot weather, when incidences of polio were highest. This resulted in a general fear that polio could be caught from any body of water. People were advised to stay away from crowded places,

Jantzen.

if you care how you look in a swim suit

the silken touch... the dream fabric of all time, lavishly slubbed with silk and designedly two-faced, the surface elegantly Italiamate, the inside smooth and soft and loving. Jantzen does it in fabulous new swim suits with famous Jantzen shaping-genius to make you look as wonderful as you feel. Right, "silk sylph" with marvelous Jantzen built-in bra 18.95... left, "roman empire", square decolletage back and front and the Jantzen-exclusive French bra cups that uplift and separate divinely 19.95... swim caps to match 1.98

525 MINUTES TO ROME VIA PAN AMERICAN JET CLIPPER*...2 MINUTES TO GLOBAL GLAMOUR VIA JAN'

and epidemics in the 1940s and early 50s often meant swimming pools were closed. But, according to the British Polio Fellowship, there was never any real risk of infection from chlorinated water. Those who had contracted the virus, meanwhile, were banned from swimming pools until 1952, even though once the early stage of infection has passed, a polio-disabled person carries no more polio-virus than anyone else. When the Association of Baths Superintendents finally lifted the ban, the movement that led to disabled people taking part in all levels of swimming up to the Paralympic Games began.

One former lifeguard remembers a polio scare at the Parliament Hill Lido in the mid 1950s, 'people stopped coming. It was empty, attendance really dropped off.' But most of the time there was a holiday camp atmosphere. 'It was a safe and lively place, there was never any violence,' says Murray, 'it was just very boisterous. We were like wild kids and the lido was our territory.'

There was still plenty of showing off at the nation's lidos in the 1950s, with water polo competitions and synchronized swimming displays and, around the poolside, Morris dancers and bathing beauty contests. Many lidos were used as film sets, while some hired entertainers like north Londoner Roy Fransen, a high diver and stuntman who set himself – and the water surface – alight with petrol. For the Queen's Coronation in 1953 local schools were given a day's holiday and children in Ruislip were given a teaspoon, a commemorative mug and a free coupon to the lido.

The Parliament Hill Lido held many summer swimming galas and diving competitions in the 1950s, such as the County of London Championships. Spectators entered from the back of the building and stood to watch along the terraces. The galas were festive events and well ordered, with tables set out and officials walking from end to end. But to Murray's annoyance, swimming wasn't allowed on such days and sometimes he would run and take a quick dip during a lull in proceedings.

In the 1950s, around 100,000 people visited the Parliament Hill Lido each year, and not just children but elderly bathers. Roy Naisbitt, who sometimes went on cold winter's mornings, remembers seeing Great War veterans washing themselves with domestic scrubbing brushes and cheap bars of Sunlight soap. On hot summer nights, Naisbitt and his friends would climb the wall at the fountain end and skinny dip. Then the authorities laid rolls of barbed wire along the walls and this, along with the cold water, meant 'some people referred to the lido as "Coldtits", after the German World War II prison Colditz.'

Left There was still plenty of showing off at the nation's lidos in the 50s; a Jantzen advert from *Life* magazine in 1959

8. The Swinging 60s and 70s

... the wan
Sun manages to strike such tin glints
From the linked ponds that my eyes wince
And brim; the city melts like sugar
Sylvia Plath, from 'Parliament Hill Fields', 1961

The 1960s saw the beginning of major changes at all four swimming spots on Hampstead Heath, coinciding with yet another transfer in management. In 1965 the Greater London Council replaced the LCC, covering a far wider area than its predecessor and sharing responsibilities for providing leisure services with local boroughs. In 1966 it laid down new regulations for the thirteen places then available for open-air bathing: three lidos, eight swimming baths and the three ponds on Hampstead Heath. The rules covered everything from opening hours and fees, to acceptable swimwear and designated places to sunbathe. It was the latter two that would cause the most conflict. Bathers at all three ponds were supposed to wear costumes or trunks 'of such size and texture as to not offend against public decency,' according to GLC regulations. But public decency was to be offended by ever more revealing costumes; by the fact that suntans were more fashionable than ever, and by a renewed interest in nudism.

The Mixed Pond

At the Mixed Pond, charges had now increased; after 10 a.m. adults paid two shillings, and children paid sixpence. Regulated hours remained unfairly segregated, with only men and boys allowed in the early mornings when entrance was still free. Mike King, who found fame as part of the British pop trio The King Brothers, remembers the raft being so crowded that the lifeguards couldn't see if anyone was in trouble. Margaret Hepburn recalls the pond on one hot summer's night, 'It was about 10 p.m. and it was teeming with people, there were people everywhere and they couldn't do anything about it. A large middle-aged woman took off everything but her bra and pants and jumped in. People were queuing up for the board and a dog was there too. It waited for its turn, dived in, came out on the bank, and took its place in the queue again.'

In 1961 the pond became home to an animal of another kind when Alberto Cavalcanti chose it as the setting for his black and white classic *The Monster of Highgate Ponds*, in which a boy receives a mysterious egg from his explorer uncle. The egg hatches into a pre-historic dragon, which takes to the waters of the Mixed Pond and terrifies the locals before being removed to the docks and sent back to Indonesia.

In the 1960s the Hampstead Swimming Club continued to hold competition events at the Mixed Pond, with a busy list of fixtures from April to December. There were also novelty races – club members sometimes swam with lit candles – a clothes race and diving contests, as well as the annual race against the Highgate Life-Buoys. In 1969 the Hampstead Club issued a jubilee membership card and held a dinner dance, but after half a century of existence it wound up shortly afterwards. 'All the fathers gradually died off,' explains Tony Duthie, 'and all the sons couldn't afford to buy houses in Hampstead and moved to the suburbs.' The youngsters who were left 'decided it wasn't the life for them, going into cold water and so forth,' says Mickey Rooney, 'We ended up with about six people on a Sunday morning and in the summer we had to be out when people paid to come in, so in the end we shut the club.'

However the pond was still host to one champion swimmer, 'King of the Channel' Kevin Murphy, who has swum the Channel thirty four times, more than any man in history. In 1970 he became the first amateur and the first Briton to accomplish a two-way Channel swim, and the same year set a world record for swimming from Northern Ireland

Left 'King of the Channel' Kevin Murphy learnt to acclimatize to cold water by training at the Mixed Pond. Here, he is posing at the Men's Pond, circa 1970

FIXTURES 1963

CONSISTENCY COMPETITION — Points are awarded to Members during the period from January 1st, 1962 to December 25th, 1962 (including Xmas Day Trophies)

AUSTIN MEMORIAL TROPHY

Four Points, Winner of Race; three Points, Second in Race; two Points, Third in Race; and one Point, Starting in Race; also one Point for attendance by 9 a.m. during Summer-time and 9.30 a.m. during Winter months.

Competitors who are winners of Trophies are not to receive points for winning a race, only a point for starting in the race and a point for attendance.

1st Prize will be given for every race, except Trophy Races when there will be Trophy and two prizes

Date 1963		Event	Winner	Date 1963		Event	Winner
April	7	50 yds. Time Trial		July	28	Plunge Handicap	
"	21	50 yds. Handicap		Aug.	11	Medley Handicap—55 Back, 55 Breast, 110 Free	
"	28	50 yds. Handicap "Mrs. Reed Trophy"		"	18	Clothes Race Handicap	
May	5	50 yds. Handicap "Mr. Reed Trophy"		"	25	Novelty Race Handicap	
"	12	110 yds. Handicap "Mr. Reed Trophy"		Sept.	1	Seniors versus Juniors Team Race Handicap	
"	19	220 yds. Sealed Handicap "Mr. Reed Trophy"		"	8	110 yds. Pairs Race	
"	26	55 yds. Junior Handicap "Lusty Trophy" and Novelty Race		"	15	110 yds. Handicap	
June	9	55 yds. Breaststroke Handicap ...		"	22	50 yds. Pairs Handicap	
"	16	55 yds. Junior Handicap "Lusty Trophy" and Novelty Race		"	29	Veterans Handicap and "Novelty Race"	
"	23	55 yds. Pairs Handicap ...		Oct.	6	50 yds. Scratch Team Trial ...	
"	30	55 yds. Junior Handicap "Lusty Trophy" and Novelty Race		"	13	Annual Race versus Highgate ...	
July	7	440 yds. Sealed Handicap "Hiley-Wood Trophy"		"	20	50 yds. Handicap	
"	14	110 yds. Pairs Race		Dec.	25	XMAS DAY RACE (Handicap) Seniors 50 yds.	
"	21	880 yds. Sealed Handicap "Davies Trophy"				Webster and MacNamara Cups	
						Juniors 50 yds.	
						Chipperfield and Spring Cups	

Above A Hampstead Swimming Cub fixture list; six years later, after fifty years of existence, the club closed

to Scotland, a title he held for eighteen years. 'I started swimming at the Mixed Pond in 1963 when I was fourteen,' he remembers, 'and that happened to be the worst winter on record. I was a member of the Kingsbury Swimming Club and a man called Watts was our coach. He was involved in the Hampstead Club and he suggested I go to the pond. I wasn't used to cold water and it was a shock to the system. But the club members had a way of doing it, they used to run around and play football in the changing room first to warm themselves up. The Mixed Pond is where I first acclimatized to cold water and when I swam Loch Ness in 1976 it was cold but I could cope with it.'

Below The 1963 Christmas Day line up at the Mixed Pond

The Highgate Men's Pond

In the 1960s the Men's Pond still had the longest opening hours and entrance remained free, although swimmers were expected to use a locker for their clothes, which cost tuppence. Sunbathing was officially restricted to the dressing enclosure. The GLC was also worried about the potential dangers of diving; the two upper platforms were only to be used by experienced divers and 'entirely at their own risk'. The pond still attracted Channel swimmers, and year round bathers, like seventy seven-year-old Labour MP Hector Hughes. He told the press that an MP's life was not a healthy one – too much overcrowding, not enough air or exercise – and the remedy was simple: move Parliament to an open-air site on Hampstead Heath. Hughes had a soft spot for the Heath, marching across it every morning to the Men's Pond for a keep-fit swim. 'After that,' he told the press, 'I can just about survive a day at the House.' Another regular was historian and academic A.J.P. Taylor, who remained a summer swimmer for the next two decades.

The enclosure at the Men's Pond was still packed with boxers and weightlifters. Several famous boxers trained here in the 1970s, many under the auspices of George Francis, including Bunny Sterling, Cornelius Boza Edwards, Frank Bruno and John Conteh. When Francis died in 2002, an obituary described him as 'the tough and colourful Londoner, whose Spartan methods, including midwinter plunges into the icy waters of Highgate Pond, became legendary in the sport.'

Conteh started going to the pond when he turned professional in 1971. 'The idea was George's, he'd been using it as a training ground well before I knew him, and when you turn pro you just follow what the manager says. But I felt it was a special place because although the run over the Heath was rugged, the scenery was beautiful, particularly running past Kenwood House, which seemed odd because we were there among that beauty training to destroy, and to be able to afford the same beautiful things. George had us doing various exercises in the enclosure, with weights, sit ups, and a medicine ball, then afterwards he would have us jump into the pond, even if we had to break the ice to do it. I loved it because of the discipline and the challenge – don't ask questions just respond fast – and because this type of action will help you win the fight. People get to The Championship from many different places, mine happened to be the pond.'

Right Trainer George Francis flanked by John Conteh (left) and Bunny Johnson (right) about to take a dip in the Men's Pond, March 1975. The shot was dreamt up by Francis for publicity purposes

In the 60s and 70s the Men's Pond also gained a reputation as a gathering place for the gay community, much to the horror of the homophobes. One ex-lifeguard insists, 'It started in the 60s with the white polo necked brigade. A scout came in from the Spaniards Inn area and he cruised around and after that the gays started coming in and it changed quite a bit.' But the pond had been known, to some extent, as a gay friendly place since at least the 1950s. 'There were quite a few openly gay men, like Freddy the pianist who used to kiss the back of your hand and say you've made my day,' recalls one swimmer, 'And there were always a lot of body beautiful boys stretching and showing off'. Hampstead Heath had long been known as a cruising ground. As early as 1904, a letter writer complained to the press about 'indecent use of the Heath at dusk' when 'amorous couples' – presumably heterosexual – gathered as soon as it got dark. 'It is impossible to walk across the grass without witnessing scores of sights which would disgrace the lowest race of savages … a few arrests should stay the plague.'

Left Sunbathing in the Men's Pond enclosure in the early 1960s

The Heath had also been a cruising ground for gay men since the nineteenth century. The King William IV pub in Hampstead, often described as one of the oldest gay pubs in London, turned 'discreetly gay' in the late 1930s, specifically to cater for men visiting the Heath, when its fame quickly eclipsed older cruising grounds such as Hyde Park and Clapham Common. But male homosexuality remained illegal until 1967, when it was decriminalised in England and Wales, and even then discrimination was rife. There were frequent attacks on gay men in parks, as well as harassment by wardens. To openly show another man affection meant controversy, or violence. But the following years would see enormous strides in gay rights. In 1970 the Gay Liberation Front was formed in London, and the first 'Gay Day' held in Hyde Park, and in the decades to come the Highgate Men's Pond would become one of the most famous gay spots in the country.

The Kenwood Ladies' Pond

In the 1960s and 70s the Kenwood Ladies' Pond still had shorter hours than the men's, and on winter mornings it was only open for three hours. Again swimmers were expected to store their belongings, this time in baskets that cost sixpence, three times that of the lockers at the Men's Pond. Younger swimmers now had to prove their proficiency, as Vicky Cornwell remembers. 'You had to have a certificate from school that you had done a width and could swim. I struggled to get it, but then when I was eleven I was allowed in. Lifeguard Kingy put me in on a rope with lumps of cork on it; I had to swim from step to step to prove I was confident in the water. And after that she let me swim in the pond.'

Many of today's swimmers first discovered the pond in the 60s. 'It was a beautiful place and not very busy,' says Janet Richardson, 'I only went in summer and there were a lot of young women like me working in London. It was a wonderful lifeline.' Margaret Dickinson remembers being quite frightened by the cohort of tough old women, the pensioners who swam in winter. The pond was popular among 'teachers and struggling people', although there were also some well-known faces such as Labour MP Edith Summerskill, who later became Baroness Summerskill of Kenwood.

In the 60s and 70s the pond also became known, not entirely accurately, as a gathering place for lesbians. One swimmer remembers being told it was 'for lesbians only', while another recalls the year 'a rumour went round that the bank was 'full of lesbians' and some mothers forbade their daughters to go there – incredible, but true.' But the pond was a place where women could meet without fear of harassment, at a time when isolation was a major problem and when there were only half a dozen gay clubs and bars in London. Peace activist Pat Arrowsmith, the first woman to 'come out' in *Who's Who*, says there were 'a fair number of lesbians at the Women's Pond, it's common sense, all women and all female staff means it will be a gay place. I don't want to exaggerate this intimation of a lesbian subculture but I was approached a couple of times, I became involved with one woman and became good friends with the other. But I never went there to make a pick up.'

Most women still chose the pond for its sense of seclusion. 'I used to walk past the Mixed Pond but I never fancied that one,' remembers Margaret Drabble, 'The Ladies' Pond was so charming and private and secret, whereas at the Mixed Pond the whole world sees you. And it was a rather nice thing that children weren't allowed in. I love children, and I had three myself, but I was jolly pleased they weren't allowed in. The Ladies' Pond was very grown up and on a beautiful summer's day it was a special thing to do. The lane was very pretty and magical and the pond looked like an oil painting. The water was wonderful, clear and silky and cool, and there were all these moorhens. Some days you could hardly lie down there were so many people and it was very hippy like. Women wore bead necklaces and not much else, people were quite colourful then and I liked that. It wasn't anarchic but it had a free feel to it and that was part of the period. I don't remember any interventions or quarrels, except when it was so crowded that people shoved others off their picnic space.'

In the 70s there were about ten early morning swimmers, and lifeguards had nicknames for them, like 'Underwater Barbara' and 'BBC Ann'. One regular, an eighty-year-old woman known as 'The Baroness', would arrive at the pond in the winter dark, put on her costume and comb her long grey hair, before descending down the ladder. Pat Latchford, who became a lifeguard in 1958, remembers, 'She floated in the water doing the yoga lotus

Below Peace activist Pat Arrowsmith pictured at the Ladies' Pond in September 2010

position and I would pray, "Please God don't let her die". Then she got out, I made her some instant porridge, and she left. I never knew her name, but I think she was German or Austrian. She would give me half a date all wrapped up in a tiny bit of brown paper and say, "Here you go dear". She came quite regularly and one morning I found her sitting on the path, all curled up, waiting to come in.'

May Allan was another year-round swimmer. 'I spent all my time at the pond; it was the only place I could escape. In the winter we would sit on the old springboard, or up on the tower, drinking tea and laughing.' The women did tap dancing together and played boules. Then one day Allan had a surprise, 'I saw a woman coming out after a swim in the pond and I said to Pat the lifeguard, "that looks like Katharine Hepburn". And Pat said, "It is Katharine Hepburn!" She always said good morning, although she never stopped to chat. She was in her sixties or seventies and she looked so ordinary. I only recognized her by her smile.' Latchford remembers the day Hepburn went up the 10ft springboard because a young girl was too nervous to dive, 'she dived to show the girl how to do it and how to be brave and then the girl dived too, well she had to didn't she?' Hepburn, who was born in 1907, had recently won an Academy Award for *Guess Who's Coming to Dinner*.

Swimming and diving aside, many women still came to the pond just to sunbathe, which was officially restricted to the grass area behind the dressing shelter. And they flagrantly disregarded the rules on costumes as Jeanne Castree Symonds, who discovered the pond in the early 1970s, remembers, 'It was a very calm place; there were no men and no one acting in a predatory way. The pond had a green feel to it; it was very different from a swimming pool with lovely soft water. There were a lot of old ladies, some in their eighties and someone told me they were the Highgate Ladies Group. Everyone seemed older than us and the pond felt quite exclusive. The swimmers were keen and they wore unfashionable costumes and hats with rubber straps under the chin. You had to be serious to be swimming in the Ladies' Pond. But sunbathing was the big thing. It was quite secluded, and you needed a private place to sunbathe. There was a woman in charge and we thought she was a bit of a dragon, but then we were flighty young girls. She would patrol the meadow saying, "turn over ladies, turn over ladies". So some people crocheted nipple covers. They were the size of a half crown, maybe smaller, and shaped like a daisy. Women wore them so they could say they weren't topless. The daisy was the Mary Quant symbol and the logo was everywhere on make-up and everything. I remember one woman, she was blatant about sunbathing topless and she got away with it. It was daring and fashionable and outrageous in the 70s. But we didn't sunbathe topless, or I don't think we ever did.'

But plenty of other women did. Arrowsmith remembers, 'I started swimming at the Ladies' Pond in the 1970s. Someone working on *Peace News* was talking about it, so I took my motor scooter and nipped over. I often used to strip down and sunbathe. We changed on the bank and I remember once staggering up and showing myself quite unintentionally and the lifeguard was quite unpleasant about it.'

In the long hot summer of 1976 the GLC finally caved in and overturned the ban on topless sunbathing. However, the following year it was back in place. But Latchford remembers very few problems with visitors, even if they were topless. 'Most people were sensible, although the raft was quite dangerous, but I never lost anyone. Some could be stupid and forget it was deep. I used to frighten people when they first came to the pond, I told them, "it's 15ft, there's a mud bottom, and you can't see a thing".' Latchford also had to warn bathers about resident pike. One day a young woman was sitting on the edge near the deck, 'waggling her feet in the water and I told her, "Don't do that darling, there's pike in there." She just laughed. Then there was all this screaming and blood and she'd been bitten. I cleaned her up and disinfected her feet.'

In 1972 Latchford was joined by an assistant, Vera Davies, who had first swum at the pond when she was fourteen. 'Vera was the more social one,' says Latchford, 'she was the social hostess while I stayed in the background.' Their hours were long, having to first open all the gates around Kenwood, and in summer they were sometimes on their own until 9 p.m. They were also supposed to wear the regulation white coat, although Latchford only put it on 'if I saw a keeper coming down the path to see if we were skiving.'

In the winter she swam two or three times a week – 'if you're a lifeguard there's no point if you can't take what others are taking' – and when the water was frozen she would walk over the entire pond, 'just for the fun of it.' Davies would put the chain round the gate, but left it unlocked so people 'in the know' could come in earlier. The attendants also worked as keepers, doing maintenance work on the meadows, and they made the lifeguards' hut homely, putting up curtains and painting the walls. They installed a calorgas stove and

made tea and Bovril for winter swimmers, provided buckets of hot water for frozen feet, and held a party to mark the opening and closing of the season. Latchford and Davies also provided a much-needed listening ear for bathers. 'Women would sit there and pour out their woes and miseries, home troubles, kid troubles, stray husbands, and we just listened to them,' remembers Latchford, 'we were a captive audience. The pond was a respite; it was a saviour for many many people and probably still is today.'

The two attendants also had to deal with occasional 'flashers'. Davies would say, 'excuse me, the toilets are up there', while Latchford's response was, 'it'll fall off if you do that again' or 'I've seen it all before, duck, put it away'. Although the pond was far more secluded than it had been in the early years, this didn't stop men and boys from trying to get in. 'Sometimes there were chaps hooting through the railings, whistling and shouting,' says Latchford, 'I couldn't be bothered with them. I needed to keep my eyes on the water, not spend my time chasing yobbos. Some were just misguided, a man might wander through the gate and down the path and I'd say, 'Sorry sir, it's ladies only, but you can go through if you keep your eyes ahead.'

9.
The Lido in the 60s and 70s

The Parliament Hill Lido was as busy as ever in the early 1960s, with championships, galas and diving displays, and coaches offering swimming lessons. Families came for a day out, local children continued to sneak in, teenagers chatted each other up, and lifeguards posed on the poolside. Opening hours were generous, from 6.30 a.m. to 9 p.m. in the summer, with entrance still free until 9.45 a.m. After that it was two shillings for adults and sixpence for children – the same as at the Mixed Pond. Yet still many people didn't know how to swim. 'This country is surrounded by water (but) only about half of the population are swimmers,' noted the Amateur Swimming Association. In Britain drowning was the second main cause of death by accident, after car accidents, with around 700 deaths a year.

Despite this, lidos across the country were still used for all sorts of events in the 60s, from underwater hockey matches to wedding receptions and birthday parties. Ruislip Lido was chosen as the setting for Cliff Richard's 1961 comedy musical *The Young Ones*, and it was here that Jehovah Witnesses held mass baptisms, dunking up to 2,000 believers backwards into the water.

But while lidos retained something of their glamour, there remained a certain snobbishness towards lido life. Leonard Clark in his 1967 book *Prospect of Highgate and Hampstead* waxes lyrical about the bathing ponds 'quiet water, bending willows, shadows on trees and ripples … to be near one of these ponds on a sleepy afternoon … is to experience some of the best of English countryside.' But he didn't have much time for the other swimming venue on the Heath, 'There is now a bathing pool which pretends to be modern, and calls itself a lido.' However, it was not as modern as it once was, and lidos across the country were about to suffer a gradual, and

then often fatal, decline in funding. This was partly due to two government reports – the 1960 Wolfenden Report on Sport and the Community and the 1968 Sports Council report on Planning for Sport. These decided that lidos were poor value for money, and while the Wolfenden Report called for more swimming baths, it wanted them indoors, in purpose built barns that would later become known as leisure centres. Lidos also lost their appeal because of the increase in package holidays. By the 1960s more people could afford to fly abroad, and to somewhere where it was actually warm enough to swim. Who wanted a freezing cold lido when you could jet off to golden sunshine, sandy beaches and balmy Mediterranean seas?

By the early 70s lidos were often run down, staff had to deal with un-ruly behaviour, children were often left unsupervised, diving pits could be dangerous, and swimmers themselves could turn violent. Gool 'Shane' Khedoo, a beach lifeguard and national swimming champion from Mauritius, arrived in England in 1972. He worked at two London lidos, Lordship Lane, and Park Road. 'It could be a nightmare at Lordship Lane in the summer with the skinheads, I once told someone who was intoxi-cated he couldn't go in. He punched me in the face.' At Park Road Khedoo pulled out two teenagers in the first week. 'I also did a lot of arm reach rescues, pulling children out of the water when their parents had left them alone. There were quite a few near drownings because parents left their children and went off shopping.'

The Parliament Hill Lido was still peaceful in the early mornings. 'There was something almost like a religious feeling about swimming when it was very quiet,' remembers Eve Molesworth. 'When I went into the water I saw myself as a high priestess, there was a feeling of purity and a protection from evil.' However others remember the lido becoming more unruly, still with the bare minimum of supervision. 'In the 1970s when I was in my twenties, I went to the lido at weekends and occasional mornings. I avoided the busy times because I had a sense the lido was a bit more violent,' says Leeroy Murray, 'there was a shift in atmosphere and I didn't want to be there. It was more menacing and the fun of the early years had gone.'

But it was the events of 1976 that would change life at the lido forever. On the afternoon of 8 July, a fifteen-year-old boy from Kentish Town, Enrico Sidoli, died after being hit and held under the water. It was a busy day, in the midst of a prolonged heatwave, the hottest year in the UK since records began and when temperatures regularly rose above 33°C. Around 1,400 people had paid to get in, and there were 150 swimmers in the water. Yet there were only a couple of lifeguards on duty. Two lifeguards had resigned the weekend before because, as one supervisor told the press, the lido was like 'hell on earth' and people were acting 'like animals.' During the day there were as many as 4,000 visitors, while at night vandals climbed in, smashing windows and cubicles, slashing hoses and hurling broken bottles into the water.

Sidoli, who couldn't swim, had gone to the lido instead of school that day, as had hundreds of other children. Witnesses said he was hit and held under the water by two or three boys. His father later said that his son, who went to a school for 'slow learners', had previously been bullied. Sidoli was pulled out of the water and a life-guard and nurse revived him. But he fell into a coma at hospital and tragically died eleven days later.

Sidoli's death was national news; the police launched a major investigation set up a confidential help line, and issued a photograph that showed Sidoli after he had been taken from the water, watched by around a hundred people. With so many witnesses, it seemed impossible that whoever was responsible wouldn't be caught. 'Everyone knew who had done it and everyone knew wrongly,' says Andrew Anthony, 'it felt like a community under suspicion. The longer it went on, with no advance in the police case, there were stories of a wall of silence and a killer in the midst.' The press coverage far exceeded reports on two other deaths that had happened at the Mixed Pond a few days earlier. On 2 July, fifteen-year-old Everett Allen, said to be a fairly good swimmer, disappeared in the darkened water. Six days later, a thirty two-year-old man drowned while taking a midnight swim with some friends.

In the Sidoli case, a sixteen-year-old boy eventually confessed, saying they had struggled in the water but that the death had been an accident. He then retracted the confession, an inquest recorded a verdict of manslaughter by persons unnamed, and the Director of Public Prosecutions decided not to prosecute. There was a general feeling at the lido – that continues to today – that people knew who had killed Sidoli. But no one has ever been charged with either manslaughter or murder, and until 1997 the Sidoli family came each year to lay a wreath on the waters of the lido in memory of their son.

Today the tragedy is sometimes referred to as a diving related accident. Yet while Sidoli's death had little if anything to do with diving, safety fears became paramount. All the boards at the lido except one were taken down, and staffing was increased. 'After the death of the boy in 1976 there was no one at the lido, no one,' remembers Murray, 'I would be the only swimmer there.' In 1977 a new manager was hired, twenty six-year-old lifeguard John Moore. 'I took the job on two conditions. Firstly, the diving boards, which were illegal because of the depth of the water and the height of the boards, had to be taken down. People were doing what they wanted, bombing and jumping and causing agro. Secondly, I would be free to run it my way the first year with no interference. What happened in 1976 was an accident waiting to happen, people were not being controlled.'

So Moore hired Pete Morgan, a bodyguard who used to work for rock star Freddy Mercury, and 'a couple of other heavy lifeguards and we stood for no rubbish. We would grab hold of guys creating trouble and bar them. They'd be crying their eyes out to let them back in.' There were other problems too. Moore frequently had to rescue children stuck under or between the rusty turnstiles, and it took staff hours to clean the pool, diving in with cylinders using hosepipes. But eventually the lido returned to some sort of normality. A small group of people still came in the early morning, and in winter staff broke the ice with rods. Yet despite a mini revival, there was always talk of closure. 'They said it cost too much money,' says Moore, 'and I was always fighting with the powers that be.' It was a fight that would intensify well into the 1980s.

10. The Ponds in the 80s and 90s

The 1980s and 90s saw more changes of management on Hampstead Heath, and a new round of disputes between managers and bathers. As ever, there were arguments over opening times and nude bathing, as well as a new controversy over proposed refurbishments. The most significant change in management came in 1986 when the GLC was abolished and the London Residuary Body (LRB) was set up to dispose of its assets. What would then happen to the Heath – to its ponds and lido – wasn't clear. 'There was a big row and a lot of debate,' remembers Gerald Isaaman, then editor of the *Ham & High*, 'Thatcher abolished the GLC and hadn't thought what would happen to the Heath and other parks, who was going to look after them, fund them and care for them?' Various plans were suggested, but eventually the City of London Corporation (CoL) was appointed the new guardians. 'We thought City cared quite well for Highgate Woods and Epping Forest, but there were a lot of rows. The late Peter Rigby, then leader of the CoL, stitched the deal together. He was very much the man who rescued both the government from its own mess and put the Heath into safe hands.'

The Mixed Pond

By the time the CoL took over, the Mixed Pond was now only open in the summer, from 7.30 a.m. to 3 p.m. It had been the first pond where swimmers had to pay, and it was now the first to be closed all winter. In 1987 the LRB had drained and de-silted the pond, which in some places was less than 1m deep, and it was then that swimmer Lyn Naisbitt made a remarkable find. She was standing on the walkway as the silt was taken away, when she looked down to see a coin leaning against the bottom of an exposed pole. She picked it up to find evidence of the pond's 300-year history; dated 1691 and embossed with the images of King William III and Queen Mary II, then joint rulers of England, Scotland and Ireland.

Left A watercolour painting of bathers at the Mixed Pond by Jenifer Ford, 1994

When the CoL took over the Heath, it attempted to reduce opening hours still further, and to close the pond before 10 a.m. But when a hundred swimmers signed a petition in protest, it agreed to re-open it all day in the summer. This would be an experiment, however, to see how many people used it and whether the money spent on extra staffing was justified.

The Highgate Men's Pond

In the early 1980s, while still under the charge of the LRB, the Highgate Men's Pond was in a state of disrepair; the water was so shallow that the 10m board was taken down. The corrugated iron changing room, now over fifty years old, was rusty and a single post held up the roof. The wooden benches were broken, missing or rotten. But when, in 1988, the LRB decided to install hot showers and lockers and to build a new changing room, swimmers weren't amused. Peter Abrahams wrote to the press, 'The men who turn up for their winter morning swims … don't want fitted carpets, a four-ale bar or hot showers. We are fit enough to enjoy the workout under an open sky on a concrete floor.' Men were proud of the pond's Spartan atmosphere and opposing hot showers became a point of honour. When the CoL took over the Heath, it built a new lifeguards' hut, a new tiled area and two new cold showers, but wisely abandoned the idea of hot showers.

In September 1991 the pond was closed and drained, the first time it had been properly cleaned in sixty years. In the process four guns were dug up from the bottom, Smith and Wessons and Webleys, as well as a pearl-handled pistol, described as 'a real lady's gun'. The *Evening Standard* suggested some of the 'less illustrious hangers-on in the boxing fraternity may have disposed of unwanted ironware in the pond', or the guns may have been dumped after long forgotten robberies in the East End.

When the pond re-opened, gun free, in June 1992 one swimmer remembers the water was so clear he could see down to the bottom. But then a new row began, this time over rarely enforced regulations that required costumes to be worn at all times. The Men's Pond – or at least the enclosure – would now become the centre of a protracted battle over both nudism and gay rights. At the heart of this row was a 7ft green metal partition, installed as a temporary measure to divide the enclosure into two areas. The apparent idea was to 'shield' nude sunbathers, who would be restricted to the left hand side. On the right hand side, which included the main entrance and a slightly bigger area where shuttlecock was played, a notice now informed swimmers costumes had to be worn. But

☎ NEWS DESK 340 2424 ADS 340 8283

POOL SPLASH-OUT RUMPUS

THE SWIMMERS of Highgate men's pool on Hampstead Heath held a protest meeting last week complaining of the "improvement" work to be carried out by the London Residuary Body.

by AUDREY THOMPSON

The Body, set up to deal with those organisations left stranded with the abolition of the GLC, is set to give pool users hot showers, lockers and to replace the corrugated iron structure that acts as their changing rooms.

Mr Vic Hallums, the spokesman for the swimmers said: "Suddenly out of the blue the London Residuary Body comes up with blueprints to put in hot showers, lockers and pull all the corrugated iron down. It is not in keeping with the whole atmosphere of the pool.

"Right now the pool is in a very rural setting and the corrugated iron is hidden by the trees. If you start modernising it will be an open invitation to vandals and the foliage, trees and the wildlife will have to go."

The pool that has been used for male swimming since the turn of the century has always been known for its spartan atmosphere. And the 150 to 200 men who use it take pride in swimming all the year round in its often freezing waters.

The London Residuary Body is hoping to spend £250,000 on the Heath's men's, women's and mixed pools but, said Mr Hallums, the money could be spent on something more worthwhile.

"The money could be spent on far better amenities for the public like toilets, or like restoring the railings we've lost around the pool. It's not unknown for ladies when passing to ask to use our loos."

But Mr Allan Tyler, the general manager of LRB, said: "We are not modernising at all but refurbishing it.

The corrugated iron has been there for more than 50 years and it's getting rusty. What I'm going to do is replace the materials, the seating and replace the floor.

"We're taking the opportunity to upgrade the showers, put some lockers in and provide a new hut for the life-saver.

The swimmers describe the place as spartan and as far as I'm concerned it's going to stay spartan."

Mr Tyler said there was one post holding up the roof. If you give it a shake the whole of it shakes.

"We are doing refurbishments so that the whole thing will last for another 50 years," he said.

Improvements are to be carried out on much of the Heath for when the City of London takes control on March 31, 1989. And the total cost of improvements is estimated at £4,320,000.

THE changing rooms and the showers at present at Highgate men's pool. The structure is built from corrugated iron.
Picture: Mark Moody

SOME of the swimmers of Highgate men's pool, Hampstead Heath, gather to protest against the improvements. They said: "Leave our pool alone."
Picture: Mark Moody

Above The *Camden New Journal* reports on the contentious refurbishments at the Men's Pond in 1988

the partition was seen by some as a move to segregate gay men in what had now become a well-known gay spot. *The Pink Paper* reported on 'the new homophobic-inspired restrictions on nude sunbathing at the Men's Pond on Hampstead Heath' – and it became known in some circles as the 'Berlin Wall'.

The background to the partition remains confusing, both when it was put up and why. According to some reports, it was the pond's regulars who had requested it; shuttlecock players were competing for space with swimmers changing, while nude sunbathers were fed up with being tripped over. But others say the real reason was because the enclosure was being used for sex, and this was driving people away. An anonymous individual threatened to sue the CoL unless it enforced regulations that banned nude sunbathing. He complained the changing area became 'infested' in summer with 'naked well-oiled bodies and an intimidating atmosphere of men looking for sex'. The complainant, who refused to reveal his identity, was quickly dubbed 'Horrified of Hampstead'.

Yet most pond users appeared to have no problem with nude sunbathing. In the summer of 1993 CoL held a public consultation, with 724 responses, ninety one percent of whom said they were regular pond users. The majority were from north London, but twelve percent came from outside the capital. Asked if nude sunbathing should be allowed in the changing enclosure, nearly sixty five percent said yes. Those in favour argued that nude sunbathing was a tradition and not a problem, the pond was the only nude sunbathing area in London, there should be freedom of choice, and those who didn't like it could swim elsewhere. Those who opposed nude sunbathing complained of a 'decline in standards' in the compound and said nude sunbathing encouraged sexual behaviour.

The Highgate Men's Pond had by now developed a reputation as a gay club. On the morning after London Gay Pride celebrations impromptu parties on the lawn outside drew up to a hundred revellers, while the enclosure had become known as 'the snake pit' and 'the slab'. In Alan Hollinghurst's Booker prize winning novel *The Line of Beauty*, set in the mid 80s, the Men's Pond is a favourite spot for protagonist Nick Guest. The raft is 'mad with clutching and jumping, the toilets crowded and intent, the queens on the grass outside packed like a city in a dozen rivalrous district.'

One ex-lifeguard says things only intensified after the partition went up, 'there were a lot of goings on, we had to have one of us as a willy watcher. One of the staff would go in and check on them, just have a quick look in every now and again. We used to throw water over them to get them out. Then they said this was harassment.'

Robert Sutherland Smith, a former City broker and current chair of the United Swimmers Association of Hampstead Heath, insists the partition was 'a question of numbers and of conduct. There had always been swimmers who happened to be gay, and that was never an issue. But the pond got promoted as a gay club in the 80s and 90s and it attracted overseas visitors and got very crowded. In the hot months you suddenly found people from all over the world homing in on one little spot on Hampstead Heath. Also people claim they saw sexual acts that they found impolite. I never saw it

Right 'Men's Pond Hampstead'; watercolour painting by artist Martin Ireland, who began swimming at the pond in the 1980s

and I certainly wasn't looking for it, but I know people who did. It created a certain amount of heat.'

But many people didn't like the partition simply because they didn't want the place to change and they resented the resulting publicity, led by the direct action gay rights group OutRage! The group, formed in 1990, had a history of involvement with the Heath. In the summer of 1991 it set up a stall to provide information, fundraise and offer safer sex resources. It also organised condom clear-ups and protested at 'the continuing harassment of gay men using the bathing ponds.' On Sunday 10 July 1994 OutRage! held a strip off to protest the 'trunks on' policy, having earlier marched on CoL offices. They were led by Peter Tatchell, who had been swimming at the pond since the 1970s. 'Tatchell zapped us,' remembers one lifeguard, 'it was just me and another man on duty and there were 300 blokes outside. They called us homophobic.' A dozen protesters wearing only sunglasses undressed in the area where costumes were supposed to be worn, and barred all for an hour. Special constables closed the pond. The next day the press was full of images of naked bottoms.

The aim to reverse the ban on nudism in the rest of the enclosure failed, and *The Pink Paper* reported, 'Amazingly, we were condemned by some gay men for 'ruining' their Sunday afternoon swimming.' But other swimmers, like artist Martin Ireland, followed suit. He had begun going to the Men's Pond in the early 1980s, to make studies for his colourful paintings of water and

swimmers. While at art school he had written his dissertation on the British painter Keith Vaughan, who had often come to the Men's Pond to draw naked swimmers and sunbathers, and where he had found many life models during the 1950s and 60s. When Ireland saw a sign about the new nude sunbathing rules he was incensed. 'They put up a billboard notice that was a veiled threat, saying 'we' had decided nudism was inappropriate for certain users. Exactly who was this 'we'? This was height of AIDS; it fuelled the flames of hatred.' Ireland says the partition was a case of conservative puritanism and that nudity was being sexualized. 'Swimmers were asked to cover-up for no apparent reason other than nosey parker's wanting to spoil things for those wanting to swim free in both

Above A crowded jetty at the Men's Pond in the 1980s

Right In 1988 the Ladies' Pond was mudded out and the diving board taken down

senses of the word.' When he heard about the OutRage! protest, he got together with some friends and they decided 'to create havoc. We marched in, undressed, and stayed undressed. We just sat reading newspapers. This wasn't a problem because it was a tradition that had been going on for a hundred years. But men from the council came in fully dressed to get us. I said, "It is an enclosure, so if you want me to leave get the police, I'm not moving." They didn't have the authority to eject me. So they didn't do anything.'

Despite the controversy, the partition remained, except for one winter's night when a disgruntled swimmer climbed in and spent an hour dismantling it. He told the press, 'My only regret is that I forgot to leave a note to say it had been taken down by a regular swimmer, not one of the gays.' The barrier was immediately replaced. That year fifty people took part in the Christmas Day event, after which one man emerged totally naked, not in protest but because he had lost his trunks in the icy water.

The Kenwood Ladies' Pond

In the 1980s the Ladies' Pond was also seen as a perfect spot for nude sunbathing, and lifeguards frequently patrolled the meadow to check women were suitably dressed. In 1983 Pat Latchford retired, so it was left to new lifeguards to enforce the rules. At one point a peacock named Bluey adopted the pond and he took on the arduous task. 'He used to walk across the meadow and look at everyone to make sure they had their clothes on,' says May Allan.

For many teenagers who had swum in the Mixed Pond as children, and sometimes snuck into the Men's Pond at night, the Ladies' Pond became a more grown up place to go. 'It was our hangout and where we went to catch up with mates,' says one, 'us sun crazed Londoners would try to be naked. Breasts were okay, but it used to be a bit annoying having to keep your knickers on.'

The 1980s saw a boom in nudism, and Britain now had nine official nudist beaches, but topless bathing was still causing plenty of controversy. In the boiling hot summer of 1983 two councils – Bournemouth and Torbay – banned topless women on its beaches, citing ancient local by-laws concerning 'indecent' bathing.

But it was allegations of racism, not topless sunbathing, that would next see the Ladies' Pond making local headlines. According to the press, a racist incident occurred on 1 June 1985 involving two black women and a white member of staff. One swimmer

who was there that day says a black woman entered the pond's enclosure with a dog, and a white swimmer told her to leave, 'I don't know what the white woman said but she didn't have a nice tongue and word spread'. The incident was raised with Camden Women's Committee and it agreed to take up the matter with the GLC. The Camden and Islington Black Sisters Group asked for a full investigation. When it found the GLC's response 'unsatisfactory', the group led around sixty placard carrying women in a sit-in protest, supported by Camden Council's Women's Unit. Swimmers were asked to boycott the pond for the day, and around a quarter agreed. The following day however, the pond opened as normal.

The same year as the protest, a new group was formed, the Association of Users of the Kenwood Ladies' Pond, founded by Olive Paynton a JP, Liberal Councillor and MBE. The group played a pivotal role in getting the pond cleaned; as it was then so shallow it was dangerous to dive either off the raft or the concrete platform. In 1988 the pond was mudded out and the diving board taken down. Five hundred cubic metres of mud were removed, the first proper dredging for forty years. As for what was found at the bottom, 'It was probably a few old bones and lots of jewellery,' says Latchford, 'Women were always saying, "Oh I've lost my necklace!" The draining was bad news for the resident coots, one of which was apparently given a boiled egg to sit on to keep it happy. The same year electricity was installed at the pond for the first time.

Not only that, but the Ladies' Pond finally got longer opening hours, after persistent efforts by the Association and Mary Cane, a long time swimmer and then a Camden councillor. The fact that the Ladies' Pond opened at 7.30 a.m. in the summer – far later than the men's – meant it was difficult for those who wanted to swim before work. The LRB initially argued that the inequality in opening hours was 'historical', there had apparently been no complaints, and few women would use it that early. Cane's response was that shorter hours meant fewer women could use it anyway, and she feared the next step would be to close it down, much as the LCC had threatened some sixty years earlier. She also criticised the LRB for not doing enough to recruit women lifeguards. The pond was closed on Mondays because of staff shortages; it had closed on Christmas Day the year before and several times over the summer when one frustrated swimmer was impaled on the fence while trying to get in and was taken to hospital. The LRB eventually agreed to open the pond earlier in the summer and installed more staff.

The Kenwood Ladies' Pond was now back in business. The sign outside read, 'No men or boys, no girls under eight, no dogs, no radios' and this was repeated in French and German. Women came as ever to sunbathe, which was now allowed 'without costume tops', according to another sign, but 'full costumes must be worn when swimming or walking.' Around thirty to forty women swam everyday, while on hot weekends there could be as many as 2,000. Many regulars were Jewish, the pond being seen as the only 'kosher swimming spot' in London. When the pond was celebrated in a lengthy feature in the *Evening Standard* – entitled 'Privacy Du Lac, Highgate Ladies' hidden watering hole' – some swimmers say attendance

Below Margaret Hepburn at the Ladies' Pond, winter 1998

Left 'The New Century has Arrived!' Elisabeth Thom about to take a millenium dip, with the encouragement of Dorothy Shanahan (left) and Suzanne Collett (right)

Right Dr Gillian Klein prepares to take the plunge. 'A moment's reflection before the familiar pleasure of immersion'

increased dramatically. The pond, wrote Amanda Craig, was 'as close to paradise as any woman could find in London.' When she asked new supervisor Jan Hudson, a former store detective, why it wasn't signposted the response was, 'the whole point is that it's a kind of club, even if it's free. People are very choosy about who they tell of its existence.'

The 1990s saw plenty of changes at the Ladies' Pond. After a fire destroyed most of the changing rooms and the lifeguards' hut, a new building was erected, with an extra shower, more toilets and eventually a hot tap, while a lift was installed to help raise people from the water. A new supervisor, former Channel swimmer Rosemary George, was appointed, and in 1999 pond regulars came up with the idea of holding a millennium swim on New Year's Day. The midday dip then became an annual non-competitive event, followed by mulled wine and mince pies. But if things seemed cosy at the Kenwood Ladies' Pond on the dawn of a new millennium, over at the lido things were looking increasingly bleak.

11. The Lido Survives

The 1980s were a terrible decade for the nation's lidos, and in London alone eight former LCC lidos were closed down. Many attribute this to a change in government; when the Conservatives came to power in 1979, new legislation required local authorities to put services out to tender. Councils were penalised if they went over budget, so they got rid of whatever services were deemed too expensive, and that meant lidos. Gone were the days of a 'City of Lidos', the once proud boast of the LCC.

The lidos that did survive opened shorter hours, maintenance was patchy, and water quality sometimes poor. At Parliament Hill Lido just over 12 million litres a year were leaking from the pool, the changing rooms were described as 'uninviting' and the toilets 'disgusting.' New health and safety rules had an impact as well. Since the Health and Safety at Work Act of 1974, employers were responsible not only for staff but for everyone who used their premises. Lido managers feared being sued if an accident happened, and across the country diving boards began to be taken down.

In the summer of 1980 Parliament Hill Lido narrowly avoided closure as a result of GLC cuts, and there were suggestions it be turned into a depot for Heath vehicles. 'The 1980s were a bad time for money,' says

former manager John Moore, 'We had a minimum budget and minimum staff, the place was run on a shoestring.' When the GLC announced the lido would close because of leakage it wasn't clear when, or if, it would re-open. 'We are passing through difficult times,' said a spokesperson, 'and it is impossible for anybody to predict what will happen in the future.' The lido won a reprieve however, and the GLC agreed to spend £1,000 on repairs, draining the pool and filling in the worst of the cracks. But when the GLC was abolished, recruitment of lifeguards became an added problem. The lido was unable to open on time for the summer season, and the LRB blamed health and safety regulations that meant pools now needed one lifeguard for every fifty bathers.

Many other lidos met a sorry fate in the 1980s. Victoria Park Lido was closed down and the site turned into a car park. At Scarborough, the lifeguard's job was now to keep people out of the closed pool. The Thirties Society issued a report, 'Farewell My Lido', concerned about the rapid rate of closure and demolition of lidos across the country. Lidos that did stay open had tight budgets, even though some, like Finchley, had record numbers of visitors. And on sunny days Parliament Hill was still busy. 'When I took my kids it was always packed,' remembers one swimmer, 'and it was busy in the early mornings as well, when a bunch of teenagers used to come in as it was free. The problem wasn't that people didn't use it, it was the cuts. Lidos, being large, tend to be on good development land.'

Whether lidos could be saved was 'primarily a political and financial question', according to the Thirties Society. 'The pools appear to consume resources disproportionate to the level of use ... (But) little thought is given to marketing them effectively and making them more attractive to users.' The Society suggested more publicity, better catering, evening openings and special events. But in Camden Council's guide for summer activities, the Parliament Hill Lido wasn't even mentioned.

And while the lido survived, life could be chaotic. Paul Jeal started working at the cash desk and as a basket attendant in the late 1980s, and when staff opened the stiff, concertina gates in the morning and people rushed in, 'there was a real bottleneck at the entrance. It was a bit of a nightmare to be honest.' Another major problem was the diving area. Although there was only one board left, a 1m springboard, people were still diving on top of each other. Around the poolside, things could also turn nasty, with running battles between police and some users, children throwing stolen goods over the walls, and poolside fights between local gangs.

But the lido still had something of its old allure, as Glyn Roberts, who started work in 1990, remembers, 'I was a lifeguard at Kentish Town, but I'd never even heard of the Parliament Hill Lido. I saw an advert for a seasonal job and I remember walking up the main path and it felt like I was walking across a moat and then up to a drawbridge. As I got nearer I saw it was like the opening of a castle, with slits at the sides as if they could be used for bow and arrows. And I thought, this isn't London, where am I? As I waited on the poolside for my interview I thought, I'm on holiday.' A few years later, Roberts would propose to his partner from the diving tower, getting a colleague to call for attention over the tannoy. 'I shouted, "Victoria will you marry me?" She said yes.'

The lido also captivated environmentalist and author Roger Deakin, who praised CoL for keeping it open throughout the year and providing free morning swims. When he joined around thirty

Below A typical queue on a long hot day; the lido in 1997

Right Children jumping off the last remaining springboard in the summer of 1998; a few years later it was removed because of 'safety fears'

regulars one morning he found that 'the magnificent pool was at its scintillating best. The great ice-cream fountain at one end sparkled in the sun, and there was an expectant air about the amphitheatre of paved terraces.' Parliament Hill Lido was now the 'coolest swimming pool in London,' according to one local paper, which dubbed the 'lycra-clad lads and lassies' Baywatch Babes. But lifeguards had to be vigilant, at a time when there were still around 400 deaths by drowning a year in the UK, and were constantly handing out warnings. On an average week, two children had to be rescued after getting out of their depth, hurling themselves off the springboard, or getting cramp.

The quality of the water meanwhile, led to a number of closures. In the summer of 2001, police were called in to deal with agitated swimmers waiting for the pool to re-open on a Sunday afternoon. Staff were advised to diffuse the situation by letting in around 2,000 people for free, but trouble quickly started and a fight broke out on the terraces. The reason the lido had been closed was because of suncream, which people were using more than ever and when the water got too milky, the filtration system was unable to cope. In theory, water came in from the tank room, though a pipe in the pool and down to the fountain, where it cascaded out and was fed back to the shallow end. But by the time it reached the deep end there was no longer any chlorine in it. A complete cycle was supposed to take five hours, in reality it took thirteen and there needed to be three to five cycles after the lido closed for the day and before

it opened the following morning. After a busy day with at least 2,000 swimmers the water would be dirty and cloudy, while oils in suncream would sit on the surface forming a milky, opaque film that was difficult to remove.

Two years later the pool closed again, on the hottest day of the year, after a packed weekend when people had been slathering on suncreams and moisturisers. The CoL explained that if lifeguards couldn't see the bottom of the pool, it was too dangerous to allow people to swim, and the lido had to close in order to clean and dilute the water until it was clear again.

The CoL also cited safety fears when it took down the last remaining springboard, which didn't conform to regulations set down by the Amateur Swimming Association. Many swimmers were upset at the move, as the springboard evoked plenty of happy memories. 'Gospel Oak Lido is the place to be,' sang the English country and western band The Arlenes in their 2002 song 'Springboard'. Although the board was taken down, the old diving tower remained, and that year it would become a shrine to a much-loved lifeguard, thirty two-year-old Alwyn John, who died in a road accident on his way to work.

Then, after decades of money problems, at last there was good news. The CoL announced it would spend £2.8 million on refurbishments, using funds inherited from the GLC. This would include reducing the depth of the pool and installing a state-of-the-art filtration system, able to turn over 650,000 litres of water in four hours. This was three times faster than the old system, and would make the water cleaner and more hygienic. The pool would also be relined in reflective stainless steel, the first time such a lining would be used on an outdoor pool in the UK. This would help maintain water temperature and reduce water leakage – at the time 100,000 litres of water a day was still disappearing through cracks. The refurbishment work would take nearly a year and in the meantime, for the first time in its history, the lido would have to close for a substantial period of time.

But while the lido was getting ready for an expensive facelift, and the building was granted Grade II listed status, preserving it as 'a particularly important building of more than special interest', the future of the ponds was far less certain.

Left Lightening strikes the Parliament Hill Lido in the summer of 2004, just before it closed for refurbishments

12. The Battle to Save the Ponds

In the winter of 2004 the CoL announced it had overspent on its £5.5 million budget for the Heath; cuts needed to be made, services reduced and jobs quite possibly lost. But perhaps the most controversial idea was that, after 110 years of glorious regulated swimming, at least one of the ponds might have to close and/or charges bought in. This sparked a furious battle with Heath swimmers, who were already in conflict with the CoL over a number of other issues.

The year before, it had proposed opening the Men's and Ladies' Ponds at 8 a.m., which meant many people wouldn't be able to swim before work. So a group of swimmers asked permission for 'self-regulated swimming' in one or more of the ponds, so they could swim before opening hours and when lifeguards weren't present – just as members of the various pond swimming clubs had done in the past. A Hampstead Heath Winter Swimming Club was formed and it attempted to negotiate a licence from the CoL. But the CoL, after seeking legal advice, said no. Allowing unsupervised swimming would leave them open to prosecution under the Health and Safety at Work Act. So the swimmers, with the support of the Heath & Hampstead Society and Marc Hutchinson, a partner at the City law firm Slaughter and May, decided to seek a judicial review. This meant a court would rule on whether the CoL's legal advice was right or not.

Heath Superintendent Simon Lee justifies the altering of opening hours by citing a Royal Life Saving Society report which highlighted the risks of lifeguards opening the ponds in the dark. 'My concern was that if something happened early in the morning, to staff or to the public, this would leave us vulnerable in terms of potential claims. In the depth of winter, when the official lighting up time was 7.30 a.m., we were opening in the dark. We tried to keep changes to a minimum and to be as pragmatic as possible, but it caused a furore.'

Right Campaigner Joy Walter holds a box of signatures demanding the ponds are kept open and free

Lee then appointed the Amateur Swimming Association (ASA), the governing body for open water swimming, to do a new audit. It brought in specialists – medical and legal – and asked advice from the Royal Society for the Prevention of Accidents. The resulting report confirmed that the ponds should only open at 8 a.m. in winter, and that lifeguards should no longer be breaking the ice for swimmers.

Both the RLSS and the ASA have long historic links with the ponds. RLSS founder William Henry had been instrumental in organizing galas at the Men's Pond in the 1900s, while Life-Buoys' president Robert Sandon had been ASA's honorary treasurer in the 1880s. And yet now the two organizations were advising a ban on early morning swimming and breaking the ice, practices which had been happily indulged in for hundreds of years.

Then, in the midst of arguments over opening times, ice breaking and unregulated swimming, came the news about budget cuts. When the CoL had taken over management of the Heath there were two pots of money. One was an investment fund to allow it to get income for running the Heath; the other was to invest in capital infrastructure. While the Heath cost about £8 million to run, the investment fund was only generating around £500,000 a year towards running costs, and the rest was topped up from the CoL's private funds. Its City Cash Fund, built up over 800 years, made money from property and investment, and this was then used to manage and conserve open spaces such as Hampstead Heath.

Lee points out that until 2000 the CoL had invested considerably in the Heath. The original budget had risen from around £1.5 million to around £5 million. It had also won a Green Flag for the sixth year running, an award that recognized Hampstead Heath as one of the best green spaces in the country. But the cost of fifteen fulltime lifeguards (plus extra casual lifeguards hired in the summer) at the four swimming facilities were said to be £850,000 a year; and the only income came from the lido, at just £120,000. The CoL said this cost was unsustainable and closing the Mixed Pond would save £60-70,000. But if it thought it could close the Mixed Pond – or introduce charges – without a fight, it was seriously wrong.

In November 2004 the Kenwood Ladies' Pond Association met in a local church. Members said the Heath was common land, as established by the 1871 Act, and didn't belong to the CoL in the first place. If charges were made for bathing then what would happen next, a kiosk selling ice cream? What if people would one day be charged just to go on the Heath?

So swimmers launched a campaign to keep the ponds open and free, with the full backing of the *Ham & High* and the *Camden New Journal*. 'It was perfect for a local newspaper because the ponds define our patch,' says *Camden New Journal* news editor Dan Carrier, 'if you've grown up here, if you're from north London, then you've probably swam there, and they're very important to our readers. Everyone thought charging would be ridiculous, and part of the outrage was about how City had been managing the Heath. Signposts appeared saying "City of London welcomes you to Hampstead Heath", they even had livery on the side of tractors, and people thought, hang on a minute, this is common land, you don't own it! That was the big thing. How dare they charge us over something they have no right over? It was a hideous mistake on their part, but it helped people realize how much the ponds are cherished.'

It was the run up to Christmas, cold and dark outside, yet hundreds mobilised in support of the ponds. Campaigners saw themselves as part of a long and noble tradition in which bathers had fought tooth and nail against regulations imposed from above. Swimming for free on the Heath, they said, was a sacred right. 'What hypocrisy to lecture us on the benefits of fresh air and exercise while closing down our access to just that,' said one letter writer, who demanded, in words echoing his Victorian forebears, that all three ponds should be 'well maintained and open from sun up to sunset all year round.'

In January 2005 the CoL arranged a public meeting at Hampstead Town Hall, 250 people showed up and the venue was filled to capacity. The ponds were a 'wonderful and cherished tradition', said Catherine McGuinness, chair of the Heath Management Committee, but they were also the Heath's 'most expensive recreational facility by far'.

But swimmers accused the CoL of having lost sight of its role in running the Heath. Why had it supported a bid for the 2012 Olympics when it couldn't afford to keep open three 'muddy, slimy, green ponds?' And just what had gone wrong with its finances, when it was the richest local authority in the UK, earning about £100 million a year in interest just from its property investments? Margaret Dickinson, who went on to produce a film called *City Swimmers*, believes the Mixed Pond was targeted because it didn't have a 'frenetic support group', it was already closed in winter and it was the cheapest to run.

McGuinness was repeatedly heckled when she told the public meeting there was no intention of closing all the ponds altogether. When she said users themselves favoured introducing fees, this was angrily denied by representatives from the Kenwood Ladies' Pond Association, the Highgate Life-Buoys, the Mixed Pond Action Group and the United Swimmers Association. The CoL was warned that if it went ahead with its plans, it would face civil disobedience. Peace campaigner Pat Arrowsmith had her bolt cutters, last used at Greenham Common, at the ready, 'I was going to use them to get in to the Ladies' Pond if necessary and if feasible. The authorities were aware of people making plans and that we would bloody well find some way to break in.' The public meeting ended with a vote of no confidence in the CoL's management of the Heath, and an agreement that there should be no charges.

But a few swimmers did have some sympathy with the CoL. 'I'm a bit on their side,' says Deborah Moggach. 'A pond with two people bobbing up and down is expensive to run, especially when you need lifeguards. But the

Below 'The judicial review was a successful attack by ordinary citizens on the nanny state'; Mary Cane, chair of the Hampstead Heath Winter Swimming Club, outside the Guildhall

Right In the winter of 2004, during a furious battle to keep the ponds free, women shared the Men's Pond when the Ladies' was iced over

thought of them closing was terribly upsetting. The Corporation were lumbered with the decision they'd made and they couldn't back out. They didn't realise the huge depth of feeling about the ponds. People say they would die if they couldn't swim there. When the world is more rigid and there is more health and safety and more rules you need the freedom to swim among the coots and the moorhens and the kingfisher. The Heath belongs to all of us and they are the custodians. But we shouldn't be aggressive towards them. They do have the power to close the ponds.'

In February 2005 the Hampstead Heath Management Committee held a meeting at Guildhall in London. It was handed a petition, with nearly 7,000 signatures, urging the ponds be kept open and free, and with unchanged hours. Supporters gathered outside with placards. The campaign was covered by the *Wall Street Journal* and *The Times of India*; *Italian Vogue* sent a team to the Men's Pond to report on 'the war of the little lakes'. 'What is the Corporation thinking of?' wrote swimmer and journalist Michele Hanson, 'These ponds are paradise – oases of calm in a mad world.'

The meeting decided the ponds would not close; instead the CoL would introduce voluntary 'self-policing' charges. 'In retrospect we didn't get the message across properly,' says McGuinness, 'we could have handled it better, but we had to reduce that subsidy somehow, and no one celebrates the fact we've kept the ponds going.' According to CoL, lessons have been learned and the relationship with swimmers is now 'much more cooperative'.

Meanwhile in May 2005 the Mixed Pond opened for the summer season with a party and a brass band. Swimmers certainly had something to celebrate. Not only would all three ponds now stay open – although with voluntary charges – but the judicial review had just found in their favour. On 26 April in the High Court, Mr Justice Stanley Burnton ruled that the CoL could not be prosecuted under the Health and Safety at Work Act if it allowed adult swimmers to swim without lifeguards. The Mixed Pond, he noted, had no unusual or hidden dangers. Swimmers knew the risks and were willing to incur them. People were as likely to have an accident on their way to the pond, or as they travelled from the pond to work or home. 'Risk is inherent in life,' he ruled, 'and some risk is unavoidable.' But he said he understood the concerns of the CoL and their fears of being prosecuted, and noted that the Health and Safety Executive had chosen not to appear or to make any representation. Mary Cane, chair of the Hampstead Heath Winter Swimming Club, sees the judicial review as a test case with wide implications for all open-water swimming in England. It also represented 'another successful attack by ordinary citizens on the nanny state and the government-sponsored cult of "health and safety".' Swimmers felt that at last the law was on their side. And they agreed with Mr Justice Stanley Burnton who opened his ruling with the following statement: 'The open spaces of London are one of its glories … And of all of London's open spaces, Hampstead Heath is its greatest.'

13.
The Ponds and Lido Today

The Hampstead Heath bathing ponds trace their origins back over 300 years, ever since the Heath springs were leased to the Hampstead Water Works Company and work began on a series of reservoirs to provide water for London. By Victorian times at least two of the ponds had become popular bathing spots and people swam when, where and how they liked. But then an outcry about accidental drownings, and complaints about inadequate provision for swimming, forced Heath managers to improve facilities and make things safer. Ponds were fenced and muddied out. Changing rooms were built, with lockers and baskets for clothes. Attendants and boatmen were appointed. Diving and springboards were erected, as well as rafts. And, eventually, fully qualified lifeguards were always in attendance. But fast-forward to the twenty-first century and a new cult of health and safety meant diving boards and rafts being removed, opening times shortened, and breaking the ice forbidden. And it was the cost of providing lifeguards that in 2004 led to the potential closure of the Mixed Pond, and charges introduced at all three.

The history of the bathing ponds on Hampstead Heath is in many ways a history of life saving and lifeguarding, from boatman Mr Pikelsey at the Mixed Pond who in 1893 won a Humane Society award, to boatman Walter May who helped found the Highgate Life-Buoys in 1903. Today lifeguarding is more professional than ever. Forty years ago it was common to have just one pond lifeguard on duty, now there are fifteen fulltime lifeguards who work at all four swimming spots, with a minimum of two on duty at all times.

Left Swimmers celebrate the 80th birthday of the Kenwood Ladies' Bathing Pond

There are also about twenty five casual lifeguards who are hired when needed, largely depending on the weather. All lifeguards must have a current RLSS National Pool Lifeguard Qualification, which is retaken every two years. During this time they also complete a minimum of twenty hours extra training, carried out by one of three staff members who are qualified RLSS Trainer/Assessors. When the water temperature drops below 12°C, lifeguards must habituate themselves by swimming three or four times a week for two to three minutes each time, in case they need to make a rescue in cold water. It's believed they are the only swimming pool lifeguards in the country that are contractually required to do this.

Since Enrico Sidoli's death at the lido in 1976 there have been no other fatalities at designated swimming spots on Hampstead Heath while lifeguards have been on duty. According to official records, six people have died at the ponds since 1933, two of which were suicides. Nationwide, deaths from drowning have fallen sharply in recent years, in 2009 there were fifty recorded deaths and more people (fifty five) died after falling from ladders. But the Heath lifeguards' job is still tough, and they carry out dozens of rescues a season at each facility, mainly when swimmers get tired, get out of their depth, or get cramp. During one hot summer at the Mixed Pond, Shane Khedoo rescued three adults in a matter of hours. He has also seen as many as eleven rescues in a single day. Paul Jeal, swimming facility supervisor, made his first rescue at the lido in 1990 when he pulled out a middle-aged man 'coughing and spluttering and shouting for help'. The man was so grateful that for the next few years he regularly brought Jeal a gift of fruit. Since then, he has made a further thirty rescues, and last summer his daughter Jess rescued a toddler who had wandered off and toppled into the deep end. In 2003 defibrillators, a life saving device that gives the heart an electric shock in cases of cardiac arrest, were bought for all facilities, and they have so far been used once at the Ladies' Pond, when a swimmer was successfully resuscitated.

While the water at the ponds remains outwardly murky, bathers insist it is clean and water monitoring has become more stringent. The Environmental Agency takes weekly samples during the bathing season, to ensure the ponds comply with the European Bathing Water Directive, and the CoL continues this throughout the rest of the year. Since 1998 the Men's Pond has been rated excellent eight times, the Ladies' three times, and the Mixed once. According to the *Evening Standard*, which in 2005 hired a team of

scientists to test the waters, the bathing ponds in fact boast some of the cleanest swimming water in London. There have been no recorded complaints that pond swimming has had any ill effect on health, and while blue green algae has become a problem, aerators are used to circulate the water in summer, and barley straw added, which releases chemicals to combat the algae.

Today the ponds attract over a quarter of a million (265,575) visits a year, with automatic counters recording every entry and exit, but not the number of individual visitors. They continue to be popular with those who want segregated swimming, not just because of personal preference but for religious reasons. 'The Men's Pond is very well known in the Orthodox Jewish community,' says Mark Cinnamon, 'It's not why I go there, I love it for its beauty, but I am Orthodox and I can only swim in segregated places.' Muslim women also favour the Ladies' Pond, particularly because they want women only lifeguards, which is not always the case at indoor pools which offer segregated

Above In autumn 1999 the Ladies' Pond was closed because of blue green algae

swimming sessions. Yet while Heath bathers are furiously proud of and devoted to these unique resources, they are aware of the need to remain vigilant. In the midst of a recession further budget cuts are inevitable and, in theory at least, swimmers at the ponds now have to pay. A day ticket costs £2 for adults (£1 for concessions), while a year round season ticket is £102 (£51 for concessions). According to the CoL, all the income is used to help maintain the facilities.

But despite 'self policing' charges, many regulars refuse to pay and machines have been repeatedly vandalized. 'The pond was a gift originally,' says May Allan, 'so why would I pay to use it?' One year-round swimmer did pay initially but 'when I heard the Corporation spent £20,000 installing the pay machines I thought, why should a pensioner pay £50 if the Corporation has £20,000?' But some regulars do pay, either because they believe the money will be spent on the ponds or because they don't want to 'give the Corporation any excuse' to close the ponds down.

Heath Superintendent Simon Lee says the CoL aims for £80,000 income from the ponds, but even in a good year they get £25,000, 'we can't continue with that level of deficit. Where there are attendants, such as at the tennis courts, people expect to pay. The ponds attract thousands of visitors every year and they are clearly a much-loved part of London life. Aside from our lifeguarding responsibilities the sheer number of visitors means that for the ponds to retain their 'natural' look a huge amount of work goes on behind the scenes. We can't simply leave the rubbish to accumulate and the habitat to cope, and this obviously requires money, time and effort. That's why we ask people to make a financial contribution.' At present however, there are no plans to increase the charges or to take any action against those who don't pay.

The Mixed Pond

Although the Mixed Pond remains open to the public only in the summer, the judicial review of 2005 means the thirty eight members of the Hampstead Heath Winter Swimming Club can now swim all year round. There are no lifeguards present, and the CoL has no responsibility for swimmers' safety or rescue. Club members provide insurance and sign a declaration, agreeing to numerous rules; they have to be over eighteen, in good heath and of sound mind, a good swimmer, a habitual swimmer, and aware of risks such as hypothermia. Members have also been taught life saving skills by Heath lifeguards.

The Mixed Pond is still busy in the summer, with 65,978 visits a year. Many fair-weather

swimmers – sometimes even the majority – are from abroad, according to Sally Taylor of the Mixed Pond Action Group, who spent weeks gathering petition signatures during the threatened closure. 'People were stricken when I said they wanted to close it. They come to the Mixed Pond because they believe it will be a foremost swimming experience, a more or less wild, natural pond right in the middle of the city. Many come in groups or couples, and that is why the Mixed Pond is such an attraction. The visitors come, guidebooks in hand, to see this incredible phenomenon. People all over the world know about the Heath because of this pond.'

The Highgate Men's Pond

The Highgate Men's Pond is still the haunt of hardy regulars, with around a hundred men who bathe all the year round. The Highgate Life-Buoys has sixty members and continues to hold annual races, a quarter mile and a half mile in the summer, and a 50-yard sprint on Christmas Day. However not many members take part, as most are in their seventies and eighties. The Life-Buoys remains a closed club and entrance is by nomination. 'There's not a lot to join, but we don't take anybody', says president Chris Ruocco, who was once vetoed from joining as a young man.

The pond has the highest number of visits, and is as popular as ever with naturists and gay men. The Gaydar travel site gives the following advice, 'Concrete floor, so take something to lie on. If you are feeling a little too prudish to bare all why not take a picnic and a bottle of wine and join the Versace clad lads that sprawl on the grass outside. Trunks required if swimming in the pond, unfortunately.' The pond is included in the *Time Out Gay and Lesbian London Guide*, and has been rated best for 'serious cruising' by *The Observer Magazine*; 'The men's bathing pond is not exclusively gay but is very homoerotic: after all this is Hampstead Heath, the world's number one cruising ground … and the changing rooms are full of smoldering glances.' But the much-disputed partition remains in place, as does the nude sunbathing sign. In 2008 naturist Michael Peacock

handed a petition to Heath management calling for more space for nude sunbathing, having gathered 1,000 signatures, including that of comedian Julian Clary. Peacock told the press, 'this small patch of concrete is the only place in the whole of London where you can be naked. It is simply not big enough. … At the Ladies' Pond they have a very nice grass bank overlooking the pond. Here we have a concrete and metal box which is like a microwave.' However, to date CoL has rejected any proposal to extend the nude sunbathing area.

The Kenwood Ladies' Pond

The Ladies' Pond is still crammed with swimmers and sunbathers in the summer months, attracting 65,029 visits a year. It is as popular as ever with winter bathers, with around a hundred who swim all year round. Wyn Cornwell, mother of guitarist and singer Hugh

Cornwell, started swimming here sixty years ago, 'I used to swim three times a day because I just liked it. On busy days you just had to take your turn. In the winter we used to come out tingling.' Cornwell, who is 98, had a hip replacement eight years ago and says it gave her a new lease of life, allowing her to go back to swimming and cycling. In her mid nineties she entered a 'reckless phase' and got into the habit of jumping in, but today she finds it less easy to swim, 'it's a problem getting in and out; you need an awful lot of strength to pull yourself out of the water.'

The pond is still, to some extent, known as a lesbian spot and groups like Dining Dykes post notices on the Internet advertising group picnics in the summer; 'I will take my banner so we will all be able to find each other! Please bring food and drink.' But the pond is mainly treasured as a private place, where women can get away from it all and be at one with nature, whether curious moorhens or swimming bumblebees.

The Parliament Hill Lido

Life at the lido has seen a revival since the refurbishments of 2005, when it re-opened with a brass band and a free swim for everyone. As ever, people come to sunbathe, to meet friends and to spend the day with a picnic. 'There has been an upsurge in serious

Left 'In the winter we came out tingling'; Wyn Cornwell takes a dip, 2003

Below Wyn cycles home after an autumn swim

swimmers, in year-round swimming, and people training for triathlons,' says Jeal, 'our quieter days are busier than ever.'

The pool is shallower now; the old depth of 9.10ft has been brought down to 6.6ft. The fountain is still in place, but was disconnected from the circulation system after the refurbishments. The modern filtration cycle takes just five hours, and the lido no longer has to close because of suncream.

Some users however, miss the old days, 'it wasn't as smart as it is now, I loved it warts and all,' says Eve Molesworth, 'our old friend has been tarted up a bit.' Visitor numbers have gone up, with 65,000 customers in 2010 – a significant increase on figures prior to the refurbishment, although still nowhere near the level of the 1950s. The lido has also broadened the activities on offer, with evening adult lane swimming sessions in the summer and free life saving lessons for children in school holidays. It hosts various clubs, and is home to triathlon swimmers (who can now also use the ponds as open-water training venues) and to two water polo teams. The Outdoor Swimming Society runs master classes, and holds an annual full moon Midsummer Party and a December Dip. There are also plans to refurbish the café to serve the wider Heath as well. But since the refurbishment, early morning swimming is no longer free, except for those under sixteen and pensioners. Instead users pay £2 (£1 for concessions) and after 10 a.m. an adult ticket is £4.50.

In the summer life remains hectic, but staff insist outbreaks of violence are rare. The old days of physically evicting people are over, now the aim is to diffuse a situation before it turns nasty. 'What we want is a good family atmosphere and we're very good at managing large groups of people in the summer,' says Paul Maskell, leisure and events manager, 'we don't have the problems of the 1970s and we haven't brought the Metropolitan police in for two years.' The approach now is one of 'leisure policing', CCTV has been introduced and any troublemakers are told, 'You're on Candid Camera, mate.' On a busy day, when the place is packed, seven lifeguards are on duty, and in the summer of 2010 lifeguards made five rescues in one day. 'It can get rowdy,' says Shane Khedoo, 'you just have to avoid confrontation and keep warning people. Last week there was a man with a bag full of beer. I told him I'd have to take it to the office. He stood up and he was a big lad and I looked like nothing in front of him. But he let me take his beer in the end.' Khedoo says people are better swimmers now and that he's learnt to live with the occasional problems, 'to be a good lifeguard means preventing an accident before it happens and that's what we do ninety percent of the time.'

Yet while the Parliament Hill Lido has survived, many other lidos are currently under threat, or are only open a few months a year. In some places charitable trusts have been set up, and campaigners have urged for listed status. Like many other lido lovers, singer Corinne Drewery from the band Swing Out Sister, has set herself a task to swim at every remaining lido in the country. 'I've been swimming at lidos since I was a child, my granny learnt to swim at Blackpool Lido and she made us go in on the coldest days, when it was pouring with rain because she said it was "good for us". Now those of us who swim in the few of our wonderful lidos left do it for nostalgia, health and sheer determination.'

Above Swimming for nostalgia; Corinne Drewery

Left Rookie lifeguards with lifeguard and instructor Steve O'Connell

Right Children undertake a life saving course at the Parliament Hill Lido

Previous page Winter water glory
at the lido, 2005

Below Duathlon trophies

Right Swimmers begin the annual
duathlon at the Parliament Hill Lido,
then sprint to the Men's, Ladies'
and Mixed Ponds

Once a year, during the annual duathlon,
swimmers have the opportunity to swim at all
four bathing spots on Hampstead Heath in one
day. Many men take the chance to swim at the
Ladies' Pond, and women are similarly curious to
try out the Men's Pond. But while there is a deep
feeling of love and devotion for the ponds and
lido, there is now a new controversy on the horizon. In January 2011 CoL announced a £12 million dam building project in order to meet the re-
quirements of the Flood and Water Management
Act of 2010. This will include building up the
banks and dams at all Heath ponds, because if
the current dams fail during major rainfall – the
sort of rainfall there is a one percent chance of
seeing every hundred years – then 1,000 local
homes are at risk. A planning application will be
submitted this year, and the scheme could be
completed by 2014. The announcement was
met with some alarm. One swimmer was quick
to write to the press suggesting, 'The construction of an Ark might have been the solution of
first choice.' The *Camden New Journal* warned,

'those at the heart of the scheme in the City should understand they are only guardians of the Heath. It is commonly owned, and, as such, any change to its ponds should not be made without the complete approval of our amenity organizations.' The landscape of the Ladies' Pond in particular will be changed forever, with the dam heightened by around a metre and the changing facilities moved. Jane Shallice, chair of the Kenwood Ladies' Pond Association, says people still need to be convinced that the work is essential. But although the announcement caused concern, the CoL says there's a more collaborative relationship with swimmers since the showdown of 2005, and 'most understand why the work is necessary'. Whatever happens, cold-water bathers are a determined lot and there is little that will stop them, or the next generation, from the joy of their daily dips. Health and safety rules may have become tougher, but there's been an upsurge in wild swimming, harking back to a century ago when Britain had hundreds of outdoor swimming clubs. Today thousands of people meet for Christmas Day swims at lakes, pools and seaside spots across the country. There are groups and associations dedicated to, or advocating, cold-water bathing, as well as clubs and championships. And as for the year-round swimmers on Hampstead Heath, they will continue to bathe, come hell or high water.

Life at the Parliament Hill Lido has seen a revival since the refurbishments of 2005 and the CoL aims for a 'good family atmosphere'

Following page
Top left After staying over at Christine Garbutt's, friends would borrow one of her towelling robes and walk the hundred metres from her flat to the lido. Christine, in the yellow robe, has sadly passed away since this photo was taken

Top right Ex-boxer 'Mr Confidence' limbers up for an early morning swim at the lido

Bottom left 'Everyone at the lido has always been so friendly to us, and we have enjoyed swimming in these beautiful waters for many years. The lido has been my son's rehabilitation pool, and also a great place for my daughters to learn to swim. It is such a privilege to have something so nice in our neighbourhood.' Meki Maeda, mother of Ruri (climbing out), Rino (next to her), and Remi (just behind). Their brother, Ryotaro, isn't in the picture

Bottom right 'Ella spent the whole summer in the pool. Even on the coldest day she never wanted to leave!' Judy Jenkin, Ella's mother

14.
Cold-water Swimmers

Each of us comes out of the water
With a different story.
Whether we saw fish, fowl or Poseidon's daughter
Doesn't matter. The glory
Of the thing is its last fierce bite
As winter gives way to spring
And we can make our inventory
Piers Plowright, from 'Winter Swimmers', 2010

It is late November and the grass outside the Parliament Hill Lido is stiff with frost. The cash desk is deserted; at this time in the morning swimmers pay at the supervisor's office. There's no one in the pool, but there are signs of life; a pair of flip flops on the steps near the deep end, a bag of tangerines and a towel placed carefully on a bench. Above, the sky is blue, the gulls laugh as they fly over the water. I have walked for forty minutes to get here, but my feet and hands still sting with the cold. The temperature at the poolside is 9°C; within the water it is 7°C. A man comes out of the changing room in a wetsuit and hurls himself in, swimming with rapid, jerky strokes. Another man appears, pushing a bike, then a third. Half an hour later the man in the wetsuit is still swimming; the others have gone. But by 10 a.m. there's a new group of people at the deep end, while out in the corridor the air is heavy with steam from the showers.

The Parliament Hill Lido is only open from 7 a.m. to midday in the winter, and around fifteen swimmers come the moment the clock turns seven. 'They like the routine and they say it's good for their health,' says Paul Jeal, 'and they look healthy to me.' One swimmer, Terry, has only started daily swimming this year. 'It's therapeutic,' he says, 'and it helps my

Right The Parliament Hill Lido on a freezing February morning, 2007. Around fifteen people swim the moment the pool opens in winter at 7a.m.

Following pages The Men's Pond resembles an ice rink in the snowy winter of 2004

respiratory system. I used to get a lot of colds and I used to use an asthma pump but I don't any more. But yesterday,' he stops and laughs, looking up at the temperature sign, 'I wore a wetsuit. It was 9°C and I felt it round my kidneys. You have to acclimatize, to build up and get used to it. Two weeks ago the water was 8°C and a guy collapsed in the shower, it was his first time in cold water and he'd just jumped in. He had to be given oxygen.'

Late December and the Heath is covered in snow. Few people have ventured out, except dog walkers and a group of teenagers on toboggans coming down Parliament Hill. The path to the Ladies' Pond is thick with unbroken snow, the air quiet but for the occasional drip drip from amongst the trees. It is four days before Christmas and after the heaviest snowfall in London for decades, there is now the beginning of a thaw.

Snowball fights at the Ladies' Pond
Left Vanessa Baraister, Alison Jane Turner, Julie Pickard, Rian Kanduth and Deborah Oakley on the lower meadow, January 2010
Below Ankle deep in snow on the upper meadow, February 2009

At the entrance to the pond an elderly woman negotiates her way down the icy path. She is one of twenty women who have swum here since opening time at 8 a.m. The water temperature is 2°C. The Ladies' Pond, like the Men's, is partitioned into a smaller area now winter is truly here, which many swimmers resent. They also resent not being able to swim earlier, just as dawn breaks.

Inside the hut two lifeguards are drinking tomato soup. Ruth Cowell has worked here as a part-time lifeguard for nearly twenty years, earning money to support her studies. She has seen thousands of women visit the pond, some have written about it; others have taken photographs and made films. But what she's never told anyone is that her grandmother is Dorothy May, the attendant at the Kenwood Ladies' Pond back in the 1920s. Cowell looks through the window at the pond, frozen over but for a channel of water near the jetty. 'It looks romantic on a day like today,' she says, 'but you need a determined mind set to be able to swim in it.'

On Christmas morning the Heath is frozen, its pathways treacherous, like a giant unsupervised ice rink. Families attempt a festive stroll, but buggies slide, adults are forced to shuffle, even children complain of the cold. In the distance comes a bugle call, the notes of Hark the Herald

Angels. 'What is that music?' asks a German woman, on holiday in London. I tell her it is the rallying call for the traditional Christmas Day swim at the Men's Pond. She looks across the water in admiration as Chris Ruocco, Life-Buoys president, finishes the tune he's been playing every Christmas morning for thirty years.

The surface of the pond is frozen, littered with driftwood and pitted with the footmarks of birds. But from the jetty there are sounds of laughter. It is packed with people, some wearing red Christmas hats that add a splash of colour to the wintery scene. The water temperature is 0°C, and air pumps have been on all week to maintain a space large enough to race. A man announces through a loudspeaker that the women's race is about to begin. Eight women take their positions, amid shouts, cheers and the flashing of cameras. People line the fence around the pond to watch, just as they have been doing since 1895. The racers dive in, the water is full of splashing, and moments later they are out on the jetty again. Now it is the turn of the men. Fourteen take their places and again seconds later they are out with a roar. A child's voice pierces the air with a triumphant 'Daddy!' The Men's Pond is open to everyone today, with the nude sunbathing area reserved for women to change. Outside the lifeguards' hut there are mince pies and mulled wine. Two women in swimming costumes, their skin a mass of goose bumps, come past. 'Where's the wine?' asks one. 'You mean where's the anti-freeze?' asks the other.

The Hampstead Heath ponds and the Parliament Hill Lido have always attracted year-round swimmers. In the 1890s over 200 people swam at the Mixed Pond each month during bitter winters, even when it was largely frozen over. Until very recently, park wardens

and lifeguards were allowed to break the ice. Today aerators, which pump compressed air into the water, have been installed to prevent ice forming. The CoL warns of hypothermia and sudden immersion syndrome, and recommends people complete a medical check for cold-water swimming. But around 300 Heath swimmers continue to take the waters all the year round. Many learned to swim in rivers and seas as children, and while they come from all walks of life, they share some things in common. Most started off as summer swimmers, often deciding on impulse to continue when the weather got colder, and then never stopping. 'When I started swimming every day, everything was a milestone,' says Dermot Greene, 'All Saints' Day, Christmas Day, New Year's Day, and then February, the longest month of all to a swimmer…'

Swimming then becomes a crucial part of a daily routine, they talk of feeling refreshed and ready for anything, they try to describe the rush, the increase in circulation, the general sense of wellbeing. 'Mind and body go off somewhere together in unselfconscious bliss,' writes Roger Deakin, 'the blood sings, the water yields; you are in a state of grace.' Lord Phillips of Worth Matravers, President of the UK's Supreme Court, says a morning swim 'is absolutely essential; if I don't swim then I feel something is missing. You need self-discipline to swim in the depths of winter, and when you come out you feel fantastic.'

A daily dip keeps year-round bathers fit, physically by strengthening the immune system, and mentally by allowing them time to think. They treasure the experience of swimming through the seasons and of being outdoors, and many have built firm friendships. 'There is camaraderie here,' says John Parker who swims at the lido, 'the only thing we have in common is that we're very different. There is an ex-boxer, a lawyer in show business, artists, musicians, teachers, ex-government employees, builders, accountants, actors, civil servants. The big attraction is that anyone can come.'

Colleagues and family frequently think they are crazy. But there have been very few times when anyone has got into trouble. Once, a swimmer at the Ladies' Pond, who was in her late seventies, emerged from the water one winter's day to find she'd lost her memory, 'It was only momentary, she felt woozy and she couldn't remember the last ten minutes,' says her friend. 'The doctor said she mustn't swim in cold water again.' But experiences like these are highly unusual and cold water is more likely to have a rejuvenating effect. The important thing is to acclimatize yourself, as recommended by the Outdoor Swimming Society and the CoL.

People tend to have their own cut off points in terms of how cold they will go, whether they will swim in ice,

Left 'Pearls and gloves'. Winter swimmers treasure the experience of bathing through the seasons

Right Leah Jewett in the November mist at the Ladies' Pond, 2009
'Later in the day, I look back and think: early this morning I was in another element, in semi-wilderness, in the middle of London'

Below Pond lovers gather to celebrate New Year's Day, 2010

and how long they stay in. Lido regular Lyn Naisbitt normally swims one minute or one width for each degree, although she always does an even number. 'If it's 10°C I go hell for leather and do ten minutes or ten widths. I know when I should get out. My second toe is much longer than my big toe and if it feels like it is crossing over my big toe then I get out. My feet are my guide.' Her husband, Channel swimmer Roy Naisbitt, has invented his own personal coldometre, for which he has applied for a patent. Naisbitt has completed several relay swims and at the age of sixty eight made the first of three solo attempts, with the aim of becoming the oldest man to swim the Channel. But he was forced to give up after nearly twenty hours and only two miles from the French coast, overcome with cold and exhaustion. After decades of experience, and two successful relays in his seventies, he's worked out how long he can comfortably stay in cold water. At 16°C it is four hours, by 11°C it is fifty minutes and by 1°C it is just one minute.

Winter swimmers tend to walk, run or cycle to the pond or lido and so arrive already warm. Some wear gloves and boots, sometimes filled with hot water. Many shower

'Swimming in winter is like having a morning coffee';
Margaret Dickinson at the Mixed Pond, February 2009

afterwards but others, like Mike King, believe hot water ruins the effect. 'You come out and you're numb but glowing,' he says, 'you don't need a hot shower.' He became a year-round swimmer about five years ago when he came to the Men's Pond and asked lifeguard Terry Turner if he could swim in a wetsuit. 'Terry said, "wetsuit!" So I went in without one and before I knew it I was a year-round swimmer. It gives you a kick. When there's ice you're basically just swimming 25 yards and then 25 yards back. There's one man though, who swims for twenty minutes and he shakes for hours afterwards. There's another man, he's an actor and he does a swim and then he howls at the Heath, you can hear him miles away.'

Most cold-water swimmers bundle up afterwards with extra layers and some, particularly at the Ladies' Pond, immerse their feet in hot water. They then make a fast journey home or to work, ready to begin their day.

Left 'One winter I thought I would see how it goes and if it was too cold I would stop. And I didn't'; Corinna Marlowe at the Ladies' Pond, 2010

Below A swimmer thaws her toes in a bucket of warm water following an icy swim

Winter Swimmers

Dermot Greene, 53, Industrial Relations Manager at the London Fire Brigade, former Labour Camden Councillor, and member of the Highgate Life-Buoys.
'I started swimming at the Mixed Pond around ten years ago in the summer months. I was a Labour councillor and I needed the exercise. I couldn't wait for the May weekend when it opened for the season, and on one occasion I clambered in for a swim. I enjoyed it so much that when it closed for the winter I started going to the Men's Pond. I have rheumatoid arthritis and for me swimming has been very beneficial; you get the exercise without the contact you would get with running. To come to terms with a disease you need quality of life, and swimming is all about quality of life. Rheumatoid arthritis attacks the immune system, the medicine I'm prescribed suppresses the immune system, but winter swimming boosts the immune system. My hospital consultant agrees; he sees me as his star patient.'

Corinna Marlowe, 69, actor

'About six years ago I saw a leaflet about cold-water swimming at the Ladies' Pond. One winter I thought I would see how it goes and if it was too cold I would stop. And I didn't. There are about twelve of us who swim first thing in the morning and we have made firm friendships and meet away from the pond as well. We're aged between late fifties and late seventies and it's very 'Bloomsbury' somehow and very cultured. We say, 'Have you seen that exhibition or been to such and such at the theatre?' It's a quiet place and I get awfully annoyed if people talk very loudly when they swim. It's lovely to hear the birds and to sort out one's thoughts.'

John Parker, 59, writer

'I started swimming at the lido in 2004 after I'd had operations on my shoulders and the doctor said I should do exercise. I did it every day for a week and then I got an annual ticket. There are two ways to swim in very cold water. You can do like Lewis Pugh, the famous long distance cold-water swimmer, and put a lot of weight on, work yourself up beforehand, and then attack the water. Or you can do the exact opposite and attune to the water. I always dive in and start by swimming half the way across under the water. That acclimatizes me. Then I come up to breathe. And then I float or stay underwater.

I've always been able to float, if I lay horizontally face down on water I don't sink. I also float on my back, with my arms out, and look at the sky. I go into a kind of trance, it is quite meditative, I am not thinking about specific things. I think this is the alpha state, when you let your mind go as you drift off and the brain waves turn off and the last ones to go are the creative ones. My heartbeat gets very low, it goes from the usual fifty, down to forty and then to thirty, and it is so quiet underwater that you can hear it.

The walk along the icy side of the pool is the worst bit, that's when I think, this is insane, what am I doing? My colleagues are right; I've got a screw loose. But afterwards when I walk away I feel on top of the world.'

Charles Dance OBE, 65, actor, screenwriter and director.

'I first went to the lido around fifteen years ago, it was a reasonable summer and it was like people soup. Then around two years ago I started swimming there again; now I am trying to be a year-round swimmer. I think at 8°C I may have reached my personal limit; it only takes fifteen to twenty seconds to acclimatize, but the extremities do get cold. I was talking to a

Left 'I've swum every
morning for the past
four decades, it's almost
an obsession'; Piers
Plowright leaving the
Men's Pond after a swim,
February 2011

guy in the shower the other day and he said the danger point is when you feel euphoric, because that is just before hypothermia sets in. I don't particularly like cold water but as you get older your attitudes change and you make yourself do things. There is a regular group of people in the morning, some eccentrics, and some triathletes. Some do lengths, some do widths, and you see them like rabbits on the side of the motorway waiting for a break in the traffic.'

Piers Plowright, 73, broadcaster and documentary maker

'I started swimming in cold water when I was at Oxford University in the late 1950s. It was my last year and I just couldn't get up in the morning and I had this crazy idea. I ran to Port Meadow at 4 a.m. and jumped in the Thames. Then I ran back to my rooms, drank lots of coffee and worked frenziedly for four hours. I was trying to get myself galvanized, I never thought of health.

I was generally a fair-weather swimmer; I swam at the Mixed Pond as a child and sometimes went there at night in the summer. I didn't ever go to the Men's Pond because I was terrified it would be very macho and I felt like a wimp. And I didn't like lots of men together, it's too much.

In 1971, after years abroad, I moved back to Hampstead and started going to the Mixed Pond every day, and when that closed in winter I started going to the Men's Pond. I have swum every morning for the last four decades, with two exceptions because of illness and an operation. It became almost an obsession.

Each pond has its own personality. I rather pretentiously say that the Mixed is Constable – intimate, a bit murky and some would say dank – and the Men's is Turner – a huge space that feels very free and is somehow more epic.

But the Ladies' Pond is the most beautiful. It's Arthurian, you expect a hand to come out with a sword at any minute, and you're surrounded by whispering grasses.

Everyone rhapsodises about the spiritual and physical side to cold-water swimming. I just love being at that level in the water, to see the kingfisher zipping along, a fox skulking down the bank, the arctic terns that whoosh into the water, the enormous pike the size of a doormat that comes up next to you and flips down again. I got over the fact that the Men's Pond was all men and I love the variety of the people who go there; the amateur tenor who enjoys long discussions about music, the man who used be the minder to the Kray brothers, a mathematics professor with a great interest in ancient languages, a classical violinist with the London Symphony Orchestra. On one summer's day I swam around the pond twice with John Syer, the sports psychologist and the father of Scottish volleyball, and we just told each other our life stories.

I used to dive in but now I go demurely down the steps. From April to October I swim the full pond, which is 420 breaststrokes. In the summer if the water is over 18°C then it's too much, that lovely hum, that stinging quality is gone. There's a touch of the show-off about the whole thing, such as when neighbours say, 'you still swimming?' I retired thirteen years ago and I'm not terrifically sporty. If it weren't for swimming every day, I would have probably become a couch potato.'

Liz Valentine, 68, Emeritus Professor of Psychology, Royal Holloway, University of London.

'I began as a summer swimmer and sunbather at the Ladies' Pond in the 1970s. My first winter dip was about twenty years ago when the water was about 3°C. I just took it into my head one day and I have no idea why. I asked the lifeguard if I would die if I went in and she said 'no'. So I just went from step to step and didn't die. Then years went past and one October, another lifeguard said, 'Aren't you coming up for your swim?' And I thought maybe I should try to continue. And I did. I'm amazed at the number of people swimming in cold water today. There were six people in the changing room the other day. It's extraordinary.'

Margaret Dickinson, filmmaker

'My first winter swim was as a child. It was a February day and I was out for a walk with a friend in the Cotswolds. We came across a stream, with golden limestone and sparkling clear water, and the banks were covered in snowdrops. I couldn't resist having a dip. Today I am a member of the Hampstead Heath Winter Swimming Club and I swim all the year round, except when the pond is iced over. Some people make a tiny hole in the ice and jump in, but I draw the line at this because once you get in, the water is so cold you can't strike out. It is just 'tea bagging', a quick in and out, and you can get bruised or even cut by chunks of ice. People think it's risky but it's not as risky as driving from London to Birmingham or cycling into town and out. There is the danger of exposure if you slipped and fell and ended up lying there in the freezing cold. But swimming in winter is like having a morning coffee to me now.'

Julie Pickard, 53, writer and artist

'I'm originally from Canada and I discovered the lido in 2007 when I joined a project to do fifteen swims through London in a day organised by artist Amy Sharrocks. It was June, the water was 17°C and to me it was seriously freezing. I started at the deep end, stepped cautiously down the ladder, and it was so cold, my feet and hands hurt so much. I swam right along the edge as I thought I might have to be pulled out and rescued. I thought, I'm going to have a heart attack; I'm going to have an asthma attack, even though I've been swimming all my life. I was so afraid of the cold water. In the shower afterwards I was complaining how cold I was and people looked at me like, 'what?' The next time I wore cotton socks. I did it a couple more times and then I began some serious layering, building up an enormous collection of swimming suits, neoprene gloves and socks, caps and goggles.

We winter swimmers often think of this place as our lido. It's the peacefulness I crave and throughout the summer I look forward to the quieter times of the autumn and winter. Our lido is a wonderful and magical place for those of us mad enough to indulge in winter swimming, and every single time I come here I'm amazed at its very existence.'

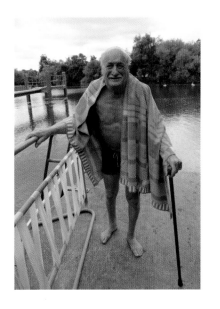

Al Alvarez, 81, poet and critic, poker player, ex-mountaineer

'I became a winter swimmer around twenty years ago and it was a man called Rudolph Strauss Augsburg who got me into it. He was a German refugee who escaped over here in the 1930s. He looked like Albert Einstein and in fact he was Einstein's nephew. I ran into him in the street one freezing December day. There was snow on the ground and there he was looking his usual rubicund self, like Father Christmas. I said, 'been swimming?' and he said 'ja.' I said, 'what's the temperature?' He said, 'ven you see ice on the water you assume it's near zero centigrade'. I thought, if he can do it, I can. And that's when I got into the habit.

I'll never forget Rudolph. One beautiful June day in 2001 we were at the Mixed Pond together and I said, 'We're blessed to have this beautiful place right on our doorstep,' and he said, 'Oh ja'. The next day I didn't go swimming but he went. He was eighty eight. He dived in, came out and had a shower, sat on the bench and died. In a place he loved being! What a way to go!'

Swimmers at the Ladies' Pond in autumn
2011, one of the hottest Octobers on record

Top left Faye Ruana by the Ladies' Pond.
'This is me in the sun ... with my mum, having
fun reading. We also swam'

Bottom left and right Women queue to get
in and out of the pond

Acknowledgements

So many people have helped in the making of this book; it would have been impossible without them. Around a hundred people have generously shared memories of swimming – and lifeguarding – at the ponds and the lido, others have provided archive images, access to historical records and previously written research, as well as crucial contacts. Thanks to everyone who has been interviewed and photographed, and to all the lifeguards who have always been so helpful and accommodating.

We are grateful for the support of the Highgate Life-Buoys, the Kenwood Ladies' Pond Association, the United Swimmers Association of Hampstead Heath, the Parliament Hill Lido Users Group, the Heath and Hampstead Society, and the City of London Corporation.

Particular thanks goes to the late Ann Griswold for her groundbreaking book on the Ladies' Pond, to Dermot Greene for his 2009 article on the Men's Pond, to Jim McNally for his work on the origins of Highgate Diving Club, and to Roy and Lyn Naisbitt, Tony Duthie, and Paul Jeal for their indepth knowledge and support. Grateful thanks to lifeguard Terry Turner for his invaluable help and access to his collection of images (and all those who have contributed to it), Glyn Roberts for sharing his impressive hoard of material and providing some of his own photographs.

In terms of personal photographs we are deeply indebted to Clive and Barbara Stewart and their niece Karen Greenham, John Neal for his stunning images of the Men's and Ladies' ponds, Michael Hammerson for permission to use a selection from his vast collection of postcards and Mike Hallinan for images of Bert Assirati.

Thanks to Piers Plowright for use of his 1998 'Morning music' BBC Radio 4 interview with Percy Craske, to the staff at Camden Local Studies and Archives Centre and Colindale Newspaper Library, and to researcher Carla Ferrari for painstakingly trawling

Top left Ruby Ridge enjoying the lido

Bottom left Benedict Waring, Joe Bloom, Christopher Wilson and Ella Jenkins sporting vintage swimming costumes at the Mixed Pond

Right Heath lifeguards
Top row from left to right: Joanne Caveny, Claire Roche, Nicola Hurley, Tony May, Luke Page, Adam Cairns, Sam Jeal, Barry Nicholas
Front row from left to right: Kim Jones, Alison Nolan, Patrica Richardson, Elly Goldstein, Luke O'Connell, Glyn Roberts.

through newspapers and sourcing images. Thanks also go to Colin Brown, Dennis Freeman-Wright, David Bentley, Paul Maskell, Virginia MacFadyen, Carol Alhadeff at Jantzen, Lyn Iglinsky, Miles Aldridge, Ben Madgewick, Jamie Smith, Naomi Peck, Sarah Dixon, Barry North archivist for the British Polio Fellowship, Mandi Skaith and Gordon Brace from Total Vintage, Amanda Joynt, Hilary Lipman, Andrea Heaher for help in sourcing vintage swimwear, photographers Peter Tweedie and Harold Corney, Leah Jewett, Shelly Wolfson, and family Bloom for advice with photo editing, Martin Ireland and Jenifer Ford for allowing us to use their wonderful work, Michael Toohig for letting us use his map. Finally we would like to thank our publishers, Frances Lincoln, and especially designer Maria Charalambous and editor Jessica Halliwell.

In fond memory of Wyn Cornwell, pond lover supreme, who passed away in November 2011.

Swimmers, staff and supporters of the Hampstead Heath Ponds and lido,
clockwise from left to right: Mike King, Maxine Edwards, Terry Turner, Tony
May and students, Paul Jeal and Michael Annegarn, Tony Duthie, Michelle
Greengrass, Dan Fawkes, Clive Stewart, group picture: Fiona Miller, Paul Jeal,
Paul Maskell and Alistair Campbell, John Moore, Nicola Hurley, Dylan Hall,
Leeroy Murray, George Gabriel, Glyn Roberts, Dennis Rowe, Shane Khedoo

Sources and further reading

Andrew Anthony, Gospel Oak Lido, *Observer Life* article, 1995

H. R. Austin, *How to Swim*, Methuen & Co, 1914

Chris Ayriss, 'Hung Out to Dry, Swimming and British Culture', Lulu.com, 2009

F. E. Baines, Ed, *Records of the Manor, Parish and Borough of Hampstead*, 1889, Whittaker and Co.

Rosalind Bayley, *To Paradise by Way of Gospel Oak: A mansion flat estate and the forces that shaped it*, Camden History Society, 2009

Walter E. Brown, T*he St Pancras Book of Dates*, Metropolitan Borough of St Pancras, 1908

Camden History Society, *Hampstead at War 1939-1945*, 1995

Leonard Clark, *Prospect of Highgate and Hampstead*, The Highgate Press, 1967

Amanda Craig, 'Privacy Du Lac, Highgate Ladies' hidden watering hole', *Evening Standard* article, July 1989

D. Day, '"A Modern Naiad". Nineteenth Century Female Professional Natationists, Women and Leisure 1890-1939'. Women's History Network Conference, 2008

Roger Deakin, *Waterlog, A Swimmer's Journey through Britain*, Vintage Books, 2000

Margaret Dickinson, director, 'City Swimmers', 2005, distributor http://www.journeyman.co.uk/ , more info at: http://www.klpa.org.uk/?p=675

Alan Farmer, *Hampstead Heath*, Historical Publications, 1984

John Floyer & Edward Batnard (1715) *Psychrolousia. Or, the History of Cold Bathing: Both Ancient and Modern*. William Innys, Fourth Edition, Full text at Internet Archive (archive.org)

Dermot Greene, 'Highgate Men's Pond: a short history', Camden History Review 33, 2009

Ann Griswold, *The Kenwood Ladies' Bathing Pond*, York Publishing Services Ltd, 1998, and an article entitled 'The Highgate Men's Pond its Early History' 1890-1930

F. W. Hobden, *The Art of Springboard Diving*, Putnam, 1936

Andy Hoines, Some additional notes on Parliament Hill Lido, 2005, http://homepage.ntlworld.com/oliver.merrington/lidos/phlido1.htm

Alan Hollinghurst, *The Line of Beauty*, Picador, 2004

Dr Catherine Horwood, '"Girls Who Arouse Dangerous Passions": Women and Bathing, 1900–1939', Women's History Review, Vol 9, No 4, 2000

William Howitt, *The Northern Heights of London*, Longmans, Green & Co, 1869

Hazelle Jackson, 'Hampstead Heath – a history of struggle', www.londongardenstrust.org

Ian Lucas, *OutRage! An oral history*, Cassell, 1998

Charles Alen Newbery, 'Wartime St Pancras, a London borough defends itself', Camden History Society, 2006

Ronald Pearsall, *Lifesaving - the Story of the Royal Life Saving Society, the first 100 years*, David & Charles, 1991

Alex J. Philip, *Hampstead Then and Now: an historical topography*, George Routledge & Sons, 1912

Alan Powers ed. 'Farewell My Lido', A Thirties Society report, 1991

Kate Rew, *Wild Swim, River, Lake, Lido and Sea: the best places to swim outdoors in Britain*, Guardianbooks, 2008

John Richardson, *Highgate: Its History since the Fifteenth Century*, Historical Publications Ltd, 1983

The Royal Life Saving Society handbook of instruction, 1937

Robert Sandon, *The Highgate Bathing Pond*, 1923

Janet Smith, *Liquid Assets: The lidos and open air swimming pools of Britain*, English Heritage, 2005

St Pancras Journal, October 1949, Vol3, No5

Peter Woodford ed, *A Constant Vigil, 100 years of the Heath & Old Hampstead Society*, Heath and Hampstead Society, 1997

Ken Worpole, *Here Comes the Sun: Architecture and public space in twentieth-century European culture*, Reaktion Books, 2000

Picture credits

Useful websites:
www.river-swimming.co.uk
www.righttoswim.co.uk
www.Londonpoolscampagin.com
www.ruislip.co.uk/lido/lidomemories.htm
www.diving-gbdf.com
www.british-naturism.org.uk
www.fashion-era.com
www.westsussexpast.org.uk
www.wildswimming.co.uk
www.heathandhampsteadsociety.org.uk
www.british-history.ac.uk
www.rospa.com

The publishers would like to thank those listed below for permission to reproduce the artworks and for supplying photographs. Every care has been taken to trace copyright holders. Any copyright holders we have been unable to reach are invited to contact the publishers so that a full acknowledgement may be given in subsequent editions.
Page 6–7 Michael Toohig (Mapu Publishing © 2009); page 26 'Hampstead Heath; Branch Hill Pond' © Victoria and Albert Museum, London; page 31 © The British Library; pages 33, 34, 35, 36, 40, 43, 51, 169 Glyn Roberts archives; pages 110, 112, 136 (top) Glyn Roberts; pages 38, 39, 42, 47, 50, 52–53, 58, 59 John Neal archive; pages 74 courtesy Mike Hallinan; pages 17, 41, 49, 57 Michael Hammerson; pages 44–45, 62–63, 80 Jantzen Apparel LLC; page 54 London Transport Museum © Transport for London; pages 16, 56, 57, 88, 93, 104, 171 Terry Turner Archives; pages 60, 65, 79, 94–95 Alpha Photo Press Agency (UK Ltd); page 64 (top) Charles Borup *Architectural Review* 73/73 1938; pages 68–69, 70, 71 Clive Stewart; pages 82, 85 Kevin Murphy; page 87 Getty Images; page 98–99 Jenifer Ford; page 101 *Camden New Journal*; page 103 Martin Ireland.

Picture Research: Ruth Corney, Caitlin Davies, Carla Ferrari

Index